THE LAST WORD
IN MAKE-UP

Dramatists Play Service

ESTABLISHED BY MEMBERS OF THE
DRAMATISTS' GUILD OF THE AUTHORS' LEAGUE OF AMERICA

for the

HANDLING OF THE NONPROFESSIONAL ACTING RIGHTS
OF MEMBERS' PLAYS

and

THE ENCOURAGEMENT OF THE NONPROFESSIONAL THEATRE

DR. RUDOLPH G. LISZT

THE LAST WORD
IN MAKE-UP

by

Dr. Rudolph G. Liszt

Illustrated by the Author
45 Unretouched Photographs
80 Illustrations by the Author

DRAMATISTS PLAY SERVICE
New York City

To MY DEAR WIFE

AUTHOR'S PREFACE

The present volume is a completely rewritten version of a book I had published a short time ago. The first edition sold out within a few months of publication and is now entirely out of print. I am particularly gratified by the reception given to my book, both by the press and by a number of persons, professional and amateur, who found it useful and instructive. This new edition includes a good deal of material not in the original edition, and I trust that the result will be found especially valuable for students. It is intended not as a historical treatise but a down-to-earth, simply-written and practical guide book.

The reader will see that while my work is intended primarily for actors and directors, both amateur and professional, I have nonetheless included sections on street make-up, colored photography, and "still" make-up, and here and there added hints on costume in relation to facial make-up. This is because, by and large, make-up is not an isolated technical process, but an integral part of the whole art and craft of illusion; or, if it does not sound too pretentious, a part of the fundamental principle of Art (with a capital A) itself.

There are a few manuals of make-up on the market, and of the half dozen still sufficiently new to be of practical value, I have little to say by way of adverse criticism. Some are clearly written and have been found useful. My own excuse, however, for adding another book on the subject is simply that every work of this sort begins to go out of date the day it is off the press; and of necessity *The Last Word in Make-Up* has the value of all recent texts, the fact of recency in itself. I believe, too, that my work is one of the very few written by a professional practitioner. I have been fortunate in my training and experience, and I mention the fact only to make it clear that my words in this book are not based on theory but on observation and daily practice. I have played in stock and vaudeville; I have for years drawn with pen, pencil, charcoal, and have painted in oil and water colors; I have been a careful student of human anatomy, of stage lighting and photography, and the science of cosmetics; while in the more restricted field of make-up proper, I have been engaged on several occasions by cosmetic manufacturers and others as special consultant; I have done an immense amount of practical work in making up actors for the stage, for photographs, for motion pictures and television. I am proud of my make-up reconstruction of the Neanderthal Man which was accepted by anthropologist, Professor E. A. Hooton of Harvard University, as one of the most plausable constructions, realizing this was the result of months of research on my part, and is on permanent display in his office in the Department of Anthropology and Somatology at Cambridge, Massachusetts.

I ask you to forgive the autobiographical data submitted above. I have included it here at the urgent suggestion of my publishers, who insist that before I release my book to the public I present, in this manner, some of my credentials.

In summing up these few remarks I have also been asked to point out to the reader and user of this volume that it is intended for constant and practical use by students, instructors, and even laymen. I offer what I have written in humility, and ask that anyone reading it who has questions to ask or criticism to offer get in touch with me. The book will be revised from time to time, in order that it will always be *The Last Word in Make-Up*.

I should like to express my sincere thanks and appreciation to several persons who rendered intelligent help to me in connection with many matters. To Joseph DePhoure, photographer, for his untiring efforts in taking many of the photographs used in this book; to Rose B. Pelser, my secretary and stenographer, who was a constant and unfailing helper; to Mrs. Marie A. Krebs, costumer, of Roxbury, Massachusetts, who allowed me on many occasions to use wigs and costumes;

to Inez S. and Helen Beulah, my daughters, for their patience and valuable help as models; to Theresa Robinson and Irving Bodkin for posing; to Carl Krebs who has been of valuable assistance in choosing costumes appropriate for my characterizations; and, finally, to those whose occasional help was appreciated at the time and whom I may for a moment have forgotten I now express my heartfelt thanks.

THE AUTHOR

TABLE OF CONTENTS

TABLE OF CONTENTS ADDENDUM 1949

TABLE OF CONTENTS ADDENDUM 1959

LIST OF ILLUSTRATIONS

THE LAST WORD
IN MAKE-UP

PRIMARY COURSE

DEFINITION

Make-up is the art of applying grease paints and powders to beautify or alter the countenance in order to make it resemble or suggest a typical or specific character. The secret of good make-up is smoothness of base, evenness of foundation, proper application of lines, highlights and shadows, with proper blending.

1. **Base.** For the easy application and removal of make-up, cold cream or any pure vegetable shortening is a good base.

2. **Foundation.** The color used on the exposed skin surface, known as grease paint, is manufactured in various shades, each shade characterizing a specific complexion.

3. **Lines.** The necessary addition required to depict wrinkles, scars, folds of the skin, accentuating eyebrows, eyelashes, etc.

4. **Highlights.** Wherever there is a crease, wrinkle or shadow there must be a highlight in contrast to it. Highlights are lighter colors, used in order to give an appearance of roundness or elevation to any part of the face.

5. **Shadows.** Every wrinkle is a shadow; so are hollow cheeks, sunken eyes, furrows on the brow or wherever there is a noticeable depression in the skin.

6. **Blending.** The smoothing together of two or more colors used, in order that no abruptness may be visible.

MATERIALS AND THEIR USES

The materials used vary, of course, depending entirely upon the character portrayed. Following is a complete list of materials for all types of make-up: cold cream, grease paint, liquid powder, liners, eyebrow pencil, eye shadow, rouge for cheeks and lips, face powder, rabbit's foot, black wax, mascara, complexion brush, powder puff, nose putty, gold, silver or aluminum powders, minstrel black or brown, clown white, burnt cork, comb, scissors, orange stick, spirit gum, ¼" water-color brush, crepe hair, corn starch, stumps, make-up apron and facial tissues.

Acetone. A highly volatile liquid used for the rapid and efficient removal of Spirit Gum and Nose Putty. Do not open or keep near cigarettes or flame of any sort. DANGEROUS. Keep away from eyes—do not inhale.

Cold Cream. (See *Base*.)

Grease Paint. (See *Foundation*.)

Liners. Lining grease paint colors are thin sticks of a slightly harder than grease paint base; they come in the following colors and are used as eye shadows and for lining purposes: (see *Lines*) white, light and dark blue, blue-green, blue-gray, gray, light and dark brown, green, yellow, lavender, carmine, crimson, red, black, and intermediary shades.

Eyebrow Pencil. Used for accentuating or reshaping eyebrows; made in black, light and dark brown.

Eye Shadow. A cream base pomade used to accentuate the shape and depth of the eyelids between the lashes and the eyebrows. Eye shadows are made in the following colors: white, gray, brown, blue, green, violet, gold, silver and black.

Rouge. The natural blush that is seen in cheeks and on lips in varying degrees is represented by the use of rouge. There are three forms: dry rouge, made in cake form, moist rouge, contained in jars, and liquid rouge, contained in bottles. Rouge is made in the following shades:

Dry Rouge. Raspberry, strawberry, light, medium, dark, orange and No. 18.

Moist Rouge. Light, medium, dark. (Also used for lips.)

Under Rouge. Used in "subduing" double chins, prominent chins and cheek-bones: comes in rose and pale rose colors.

Liquid Rouge. Light, medium, dark. (Also used for the lips.)

Face Powder. Theatrical face powder has a different adhesive quality from that of any other face powder. Properly applied it offers a smooth velvety texture to the skin, and blends rouge on cheeks, highlights, shadows and wrinkles. Known as blending powder, it is made in the same shades as grease paint and is nearly always matched, as to color, with the grease paint.

Rabbit's Foot (or paw). Used in the application of dry rouge, also to apply corn starch to simulate gray hair, and for the removal of excessive powder from the face. There are two kinds of rabbit's feet; the manufactured kind is made from rabbit's fur, formed like a paw and stuffed; and the genuine hind paw of the rabbit.

Black Wax. A specially prepared adhesive wax used to simulate missing teeth. This wax is easily and quickly removed.

Mascara. Known by various but similar names, used to darken eyelashes and eyebrows. A brush comes with this water-soluble cosmetic. When the mascara is dry it remains as set until washed off. White mascara is used for graying the hair. Mascara comes in the following shades: black, brown, blond and white. Some manufacturers make blue, green, lavender and purple.

Complexion Brush. Also known as baby-skin brush, shaped in a convenient curve and used for the removal of excess face powder without disturbing or smudging the make-up in any way.

Powder Puffs. I strongly urge the use of wool puffs, not velvet or rubber puffs, as the face powder leaves the wool puff much more readily, whereas the others endanger the clarity and neatness of the make-up, because of the adherence of the powder to the puff.

Nose Putty. A plastic substance, usually flesh-colored, will receive the application of grease paint and powder, simulating natural flesh. Putty is used for reshaping the nose, making moles, wrinkles, welts, changing the contour of the cheek-bone, frontals (brows), reshaping of the chin, blocking out eyebrows and, when properly treated, will readily combine with false hair. (See chapter on Eyebrows, p. 26.)

Metallic Powders. Gold powder may be used on blond hair to add brilliance, bronze powder on red, titian and auburn hair; and aluminum or silver powder on gray hair for the same purpose.

Minstrel Black. An ebony-colored cream that comes in

tubes for minstrel use only. The brown is used for the lighter-colored characters. This cream can be removed with water; no cold cream is necessary for a base. Burnt cork is another form of minstrel make-up, and comes in jars or round tins, in black only.

Orange Stick. The slanted or bevelled end is used in the final shaping of the lips. (Fig. 41g.)

Spirit Gum. This transparent liquid is used for the application of false hair on an exposed part of the skin. Easily applied and as readily removed. Application is made with a cheap water-color brush, which is better than the inadequate affair attached to most corks in spirit-gum bottles.

Crepe Hair. A manufactured braided wool hair. When properly applied and manipulated, it effectively simulates natural hair. (See Fig. 17 & 26a.) There is a better-grade hair known as real silk crepe hair, which is much finer and has a natural gloss. Both come in all the natural shades, and such mixed colors as gray, gray-blond, gray-brown, etc.

Corn Starch. When properly applied will suggest gray hair and last throughout the performance, so long as the hands do not touch the hair. (See chapter *Growing Old Via Lighting,* p. 61.)

Stumps. These useful accessories are pointed rolls of paper very much like blotting paper. (They are generally of French make. Since European imports have decreased, American manufacturers have begun to manufacture them.) Stumps are indispensable in the blending of wrinkle lines, the application of highlights, freckles, shadows, and reshaping lower lips; also used with moist or stick liners for the making of fine wrinkle lines. Their specific use is given in a later chapter.

Make-Up Apron. A large piece of cloth a yard square to throw over the chest and shoulders for protection from falling powder, etc. Ready-made make-up aprons of oiled silk or Plio-film may be bought at any beauty supply dealer.

Facial Tissues. Used for the removal of make-up.

White Liquid. For whitening hair, eyebrows, eyelashes, etc. Apply with tooth brush. Washes out easily with soap and water.

SUGGESTED UNITS AND GROUPS OF MAKE-UP MATERIALS THAT WILL HELP PREVENT PURCHASE OF NEEDLESS ITEMS

Beginner's Outfit.

1 Light flesh grease paint
1 Medium flesh grease paint
1 Sallow flesh grease paint

1 Medium dry rouge
1 Black eyebrow pencil
1 Brown eyebrow pencil

1 Brown liner

1 Red liner
1 White liner

1 Can rachelle powder
1 Can (½ lb.) cold cream
1 Package stumps
1 Skin brush
1 Wool powder puff

For the advanced student or group, a complete make-up box is essential. Properly protected from exposure and kept in normal temperature, make-up will keep in good condition for a long time. (I have some sticks of liners that I started out with as a boy in my teens.)

Advanced Outfit.

1 Light juvenile grease paint
1 Very light pink grease paint
1 Juvenile grease paint
1 Outdoor flesh grease paint
1 Sallow flesh grease paint
1 Tan flesh grease paint
1 Dark sunburn grease paint
1 Mulatto grease paint
1 Negro grease paint

1 Black liner
1 Light brown liner
1 Dark brown liner
1 Blue liner
1 Gray liner
1 Red liner

1 Maroon liner
1 Carmine liner
1 White liner

1 Light pink powder
1 Rachelle powder
1 Natural flesh powder
1 Brown powder

4 Wool powder puffs

1 Light rouge
1 Medium rouge
1 Dark rouge
1 Bottle spirit gum
1 Tin nose putty

1 Black tooth wax	1 Foot white crepe hair
1 Foot black crepe hair	1 Can cold cream (½ lb.)
1 Foot brown crepe hair	1 Package stumps
1 Foot gray crepe hair	1 Skin brush

It is well to know that all manufacturers of grease paints carry all the important shades. They number each color to correspond to a given shade. For instance, on one tube or stick you might see 19—Spanish. This does not mean, however, that No. 19 is Spanish with all manufacturers. When ordering grease paints ask for the particular flesh color you want and *do not order by number,* unless you know the manufacturer's code or system of numbering.

For other details and information on the selection of grease paints see pp. 21, 22.)

Now that you have read the foregoing, familiarize yourself with each item mentioned in order that you may be absolutely familiar with it. In succeeding chapters, you will be instructed as to the use of these materials, and the method of applying them.

Remember that make-up is a science, as well as an art: the possibilities are unlimited. Varying degrees of intensity of make-up must be understood. For example, the concert singer's make-up must be different from that of the opera singer, because of the difference of distances between the performer and the audience. This is only a hint as to the many problems that will face the beginner who experiments with his materials.

EXERCISE

Memorize the definitions, then have someone examine you. **Example.**

Question: What is foundation?

Answer: Reply, giving every important point necessary to show that you know what you are talking about.

Question: What is rouge?

Answer: Here you should not only state the definition, but be able to name the various kinds of rouge and their specific uses, as well as their different forms.

This over, we are now ready to take the next step.

SOCIETY OR STREET MAKE-UP

Figs. 1, 2, 3, 4, 5, 6, 7, 8, 9, 10

This section is devoted to the problems of (non-theatrical) street or "society" make-up for women.

Cosmetics in abundance are advertised and sold everywhere. If the manufacturer is reputable and well-known, he usually has departments in stores where specially trained salespeople urge the use of a *certain* cream, powder or rouge. You no doubt have noticed that each manufacturer has his "original way" of applying this cosmetic in such a way that only *his* rouge or powder will bring out "your personality." After purchasing and using the product in full confidence, how many women look correctly made up? Very few! The author "makes up" ladies for the evening and his make-up lasts as long as seven hours. Of course, dining will make it necessary to retouch the lips. Nothing else will need attention if the make-up is done properly.

1. Clean the exposed area with soap and water; after which pat (with a piece of surgical cotton dipped in witch hazel or some other good facial astringent) all over the surface.

2. Get the finest cream (tube or jar) grease paint. There are some very good powder bases on the market, but names must be omitted here for obvious reasons. Get the color nearest your own natural skin color.

3. Spread out a quantity (equal in bulk, say, to a pea) of the foundation color in the left hand. With the first three fingers of the right hand put the color all over the face, starting with the forehead. Do not forget behind the ears, back of neck, and all of the skin that is exposed to view. Keep patting, not rubbing, and be sure that the natural texture and pores of the skin (not the enlarged pores) are not covered up. If the pores around the nose are enlarged, apply as above mentioned a good astringent lotion to such areas before applying the foundation color. Ice

wrapped in a cloth and applied to these areas is also very effective.

THE EYEBROWS

Eyebrows are made up with a fine pointed eyebrow pencil. Eyebrows for street wear should be made with finely drawn hair lines. Never draw one thick line. The appearance of artificiality must be overcome wherever possible. In most cases it *is* possible. See Fig. 8.

Blondes' eyebrows should never be darkened to excess at their beginning (near the nose) unless the effect of dark eyes and light hair is sought. At the *ending* of the eyebrow continue the eyebrow in the shape best suited for the eye, in very light brown eyebrow pencil. Titians, red-heads, and chestnut-browns should use the darker brown eyebrow pencil. Brunettes and gray-haired women should use the black pencil, and more elderly types should use the pencil sparingly and skilfully (Fig. 10). Try to do the job right the first time, because erasures and wiping off of make-up result in dirty, smudgy, unclean-looking faces. If the subject is naturally gray-haired, yet younger in face than usual, a brown pencil may be used. After the pencil is applied, the little finger, used as a stump, should be lightly passed over the made-up eyebrow, in order to give this feature a natural appearance. The eyebrow should not look as though it had been stuck on.

EYES

How often have you seen a beautiful woman with pretty eyes, yet so poorly made up that the picture as a whole is ruined! Let us consider in detail certain types of eyes and the make-up necessary to place them into proper and effective relief.

THE BARREN EYE

Fig. 7

A barren eye is one without lashes. For various reasons there are eyes which, especially on the lower eyelid, are devoid of lashes, or almost so. Great care must be taken in such cases, when lining the lids. Brown pencil should be used. Bear in mind that the aim is not to attract attention to the eye in particular, but to prevent the beholder from noticing the make-up. The shading is done by adding a thin line, very lightly diffused with the stump or little finger, so that there will be just the semblance of an eyelash, definitely made, yet indefinitely seen. The line of the lower lid should extend further on, towards the optical orbit, than would be the case in other eyes ; this line is also diffused at the outer end of the optical orbit. (Fig. 42.) Do not make it a line, make it a *shadow* that would have been made by the lashes. (Never use black liner or eyebrow pencil.) The upper lid is treated the same way except that the line is somewhat wider than on the lower lid.

HEAVY EYELASHES

In direct contrast we have eyes with heavy eyelashes. For brunette, titian, red-head or chestnut-hair, do not use mascara or touch up the eyelashes. You may, however, lightly brush the lashes with vaseline or brilliantine.

For blondes, should the eyelashes be very light in color, yet heavy, apply brown liner carefully to the lashes covering them completely. If mascara is used, the color should be light brown.

The eyes should not "steal the show." They should be part of the facial ensemble.

SHADING THE EYES

Figs. 6 & 8

For street make-up, eyes should be shaded so as to be beautified, yet undefinable. Not "made-up" eyes, yet they *are* made-up. Rather glistening jewels, lovely to behold. As for the stage, the same colors are used, but the application is different.

The method is the same as for foundation color for the street, but the difference is that the color is patted in place lightly, not rubbed heavily on the eyelid. There should be only the slightest trace of color evident.

In using the mascara (which should be the final operation of making up the eyes), see that each lash is separate. Never bead them or permit lashes to stick together, as this will give them a starry overdone artificial appearance, which is not desirable.

A word about "colorless eye shadow." This is a greasy pomade sold to be applied to the upper lid and give the eyes a glistening, sparkling effect. Greasy eyelids suggest carelessness and artifice. Nature never gave anyone shining upper lids, unless they wept furiously and forgot to wipe their eyes, or in the case of eye infections when medicated ointments are essential. Colorless eye shadow in no way enhances the eye. In all of my years of making-up never have I found it an aid to eye beauty.

ROUGING THE CHEEKS

Following the instructions and illustrations on page 15, carefully study your own face. First apply moist rouge with the fingers and blend carefully into your foundation color.

For evening use, you can heighten the color by applying it a degree or two more heavily than for day use. Also for evening, for oval and "wider at the eyes" faces, the rouge may be applied higher up towards the temples, at the outer end of the eyebrows. At this point, however, the rouge should be of a *suggested* color, rather than true color density. As the cheeks are rouged, run the fingers from the cheeks upward *toward* the temples. In this way the blended red from the cheeks becomes a heightening color tinge that suggests excitement and enjoyment. A light touch of rouge may be applied on top of the eye under the eyebrow, but this must be done with deftness and certainty. Never rouge directly on the cheek-bones.

THE LIPS

Figs. 41, a–g

Rouging the lips for street or evening is an important and none-too-easy achievement. Lips should not be made up to stand out more prominently than any other part of the face. The best method in making lip-stick last is to follow the procedure just about to be described.

First, study your face and decide on the alteration, if any, needed to suggest the proper curves and bows. Wipe the lips clean with alcohol or a good astringent; dry carefully. Do not touch the foundation already applied. With your little finger apply the lip rouge, then with your orange stick, or lip-brush (which may be bought at most cosmetic departments), shape or reshape the lips as desired. Block out the undesirable portions as explained in chapter on *Lips* and shown in Figs. 41a, b, c & g. After the lips have been made up, carefully blot with facial tissue, and pounce the wool powder puff on the lips. In this way the powder sets the lip rouge. After the powder has been brushed off, rerouge and repowder. Finally place a piece of facial tissue between the lips and once more, press. Thus, you should have soft natural-looking lips that will last the evening.

Don't Overdo. Rouged lips can easily be overdone. Don't let them appear as if they would crack if you were to laugh. Let the texture of the skin of the lips show through. You'll be surprised at the difference in your make-up if you follow carefully the instructions made in this chapter.

EARS

The lobes of the ears may also be lightly rouged if desired, but not if earrings are worn.

CHIN

The chin needs attention, too. It may be rouged as shown in Figs. 12, a, b, & c, and if done carefully will never be noticed as a "trick" in make-up.

POWDERING

Powdering should be done as follows:
Blondes.
Forehead, upper lip in light flesh.
Small nose, Light flesh
Large nose, Rachelle
Small chin, Light flesh
Large chin, Rachelle
Cheeks, pink or darker flesh
Lips, flesh
Pat all these colors with a wool powder puff so that they blend, and brush the excess powder over the eyelids as well.

Liquid powder (light flesh) is used all over the exposed areas as explained on page 19.

Red-Heads
Powdering for red-heads, titians, chestnut-haired
Forehead, upper lip, use flesh
Small nose, Rachelle
Large nose, Cream
Small chin, Rachelle
Large chin, Cream
Cheeks, Pink
Lips, flesh
Liquid powder should match the foundation color on all exposed areas.

Brunettes
Forehead, upper lip, Rachelle
Small nose, Rachelle
Large nose, Cream
Small chin, Rachelle
Large chin, Cream

FIG. 1. *A young lady without make-up*

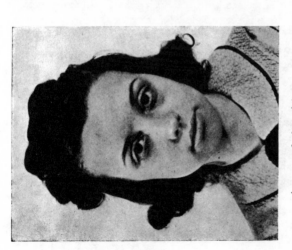

FIG. 2. *The same miss made up by the author*

FIG. 3. *This young lady's face is devoid of make-up*

FIG. 4. *The same miss made up by the author. These photos are a part of a series that appeared in "Foto."*

SIMPLE, SENSIBLE USE OF COSMETICS

(From an article by the Author in "American Perfumer & Essential Oil Review")

FIG. 5. *Best features are eyes; next lips; next nose. Ears rather generous. Problem to emphasize eyes and lips and direct attention away from the nose and to detract from broad jaw.*

FIG. 6. *Foundation cream or powder base applied carefully over the face. Base spread on with water moist fingers. Mouth given specific shape to detract from rather full jaw line. Light brown eye shadow applied to give animation and depth to eyes— keeping eye shadow away from beneath the eyebrows. Rouge applied diagonally high on the cheeks, not lower than the lobe of the ear. Powder matching foundation cream applied and brushed off.*

Plain features made attractive and effect is natural. Note how hair is arranged to partly cover the ears and how coronet balances the jaw line.

FIG. 7. *Badly plucked eyebrows and wrong use of eyebrow pencil on the eyelids makes the eyes hard looking. Chin too short. Hair line too square, making forehead too high.*

FIG. 8. *Foundation cream applied. Eyebrows carefully shaped with eyebrow pencil to bring out expression in the eyes. Contour of upper eyelid was followed ending with a slight upward curve. Separate hair lines in eyebrows pencilled in with a sharp eyebrow pencil. False eyelashes added to fringe the eyes. Waves in hair at side of temples eliminated and moved back. Surface powder and rouge applied. Although not essential, mouth widened slightly.*

A youthful appearance. Softer hair line achieved. An interesting composite picture whereby no individual feature stands out alone.

FIG. 9. *A kind face but marked by wrinkles. Loose flesh and crows feet beginning to show. The flesh falling away from the skeletal structure brings an angular face that must be softened.*

FIG. 10. *Proper shade foundation cream worked gently into the skin. By separating the wrinkles with the fingers the foundation cream is allowed to cover the smaller shadows caused by the wrinkles. Upper lip widened with a silghtly lighter than natural lipstick, being careful not to present a too youthful mouth. Light powder used on nose and chin. Medium shade powder applied to forehead and upper cheeks; darker shade on lower cheeks.*

Attractive, matronly appearance. Wrinkles and crows feet are subdued, making them practically unnoticed. Effect is natural.

(Courtesy of "American Weekly" for which the full page article was originally written by the author.)

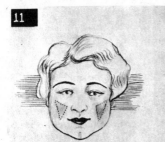

11

ROUGING THE ROUND FACE NEARER THE NOSE AND IN A TRIANGULAR FORM, WELL BLENDED. ROUGE THE CHIN VERTICALLY, (BUT LIGHTER)

11a

ROUGING THE LONG OR THIN FACE HORIZONTALLY, JUST BELOW AND BORDERING THE CHEEK BONES, AWAY FROM THE NOSE, WELL BLENDED. LIGHTLY TINT THE CHIN HORIZONTALLY.

11b

ROUGING THE OVAL FACE AWAY FROM THE NOSE IN AN ELONGATED TRIANGLE, UP TO THE TEMPLES. BLEND WELL. TOUCH UP THE CENTRE OF THE CHIN.

11c

ROUGING THE SQUARE JAWED FACE OBLIQUELY TOWARDS THE MOUTH. KEEP AWAY FROM THE TEMPLES AND NOSE. TINT VERY LIGHTLY, THE LOWER SIDES OF JAW, BLEND AND POWDER WITH CARE.

FIG. 11. *Success in rouging can only be effected by careful blending of the extreme edges of the rouged areas*

RESHAPING THE CHIN

THE PROTRUDING CHIN.

12   PROFILE

TO RECEDE THE CHIN, FIRST APPLY A MUCH DARKER SKINTONE FOUNDATION GREASE PAINT, BLEND THE EDGES VERY CAREFULLY INTO THE FOUNDATION, AND ROUGE LIGHTLY, HORIZONTALLY.

DARKER GREASE PAINT.

DARK ROUGE, LIGHTLY APPLIED.

THE RECEDING CHIN.

12a   PROFILE

TO BRING THE RECEDING CHIN FORWARD, HIGHLIGHT THE ENTIRE CHIN PORTION, WITH A VERY MUCH LIGHTER GREASE PAINT COLOR AND TONE DOWN THE BLENDED EDGES.

STRONG HIGHLIGHT, VERY WELL BLENDED EDGES.

CAREFULLY HIGHLIGHT HERE

ROUGE THE LOWER LIP WITH BRIGHTER RED

PROTRUDING ROUND CHIN.

12b   PROFILE

FOLLOW DIRECTIONS AS IN ILLUSTRATION **11a** ONLY, IN THE AREAS SHOWN HERE.

DARKER GREASE PAINT

DARK ROUGE, LIGHTLY APPLIED
Note:
MAKE ALL LOWER LIPS IN A DARKER SHADE. ROUGE, THAN THE UPPER LIPS.

TO MAKE A CLEFT CHIN.

12c
DRAW A VERTICAL LINE IN WARM BROWN OR MAROON

BLEND VERTICAL LINE SMOOTHLY ON EACH SIDE

HIGHLIGHT ON EACH SIDE OF BLENDED VERTICAL LINE WITH LIGHTER COLORED GREASE PAINT, YELLOW, OR WHITE.

FOR DIMPLED CHINS, MAKE A SPOT IN BROWN OR MAROON, AND HIGHLIGHT AROUND, ON TOP

FIG. 12. *Do not neglect the chin. It also calls for attention.*

Cheeks, Pink

Lips, Rachelle

Liquid powder should match the foundation color on all exposed areas.

Gray or White-Haired Women

Forehead, color of powder determined by the natural color of the hair before it turned gray

Small nose, color of powder determined by the natural color of the hair before it turned gray

Large nose, Rachelle

Small chin, color of powder determined by the natural color of the hair before it turned gray

Large chin, Rachelle

SECONDARY COURSE

The subject of this chapter is dry make-up. This has to do with the use of colored powders, dry rouge, red liner for lips, and the application of hair for use in tableaux or pageants.

Always remember that when audiences are fairly close to the stage they can see through make-up. When "character" parts are portrayed, as little lining as possible should be applied. Rouge should be used sparingly; eyebrows should be darkened, not painted on, and lips be made to look natural, not like two scarlet daubs framing the teeth.

"The eyes are the windows of the soul," it is said, but may I add, "The mouth is the door"? In all cases the mouth denotes character, and the make-up used on it should indicate character.

The application of the eyebrow pencil for this course will now be described.

EYEBROW PENCIL

For Child or Youth. Moisten the eyebrows very slightly with cold cream (just a film), then with the side of the point of the eyebrow pencil just darken the hairs of the eyebrow. Do *not* draw lines. Should this give the appearance of a heavy eyebrow, use the little finger to smooth down the hairs, wipe lightly from the center of the face outward toward the temple. Use black pencil for dark hair and brown pencil for all other shades of hair.

Eye shadow is not necessary, but if it is wanted, take a brown pencil, draw a short line from the end of the eye outward until it reaches the edge of the optical orbit, then diffuse the line lightly with the finger. (Figs. 42b & d.)

ROUGE

Rouge is applied with the rabbit's foot. Rub the hairy tip of the paw lightly over the cake of rouge, and with a light outward motion color the cheek to the depth of the color required. The rouge is put on the skin before applying powder. Bear in mind that color on the human skin comes from within: try to have the make-up look that way. Never rouge the cheek-bones. For the proper application of rouge see *Rouging Technique* (Figs. 11, a, b & c).

LIPS

The lips come next. Using your little finger, rub the red liner until your finger has on it enough color, and then lightly and carefully color the red part of the lips, following nature's out-line. Lastly, with a wool powder puff, powder the face from the forehead down, and when covering the cheeks keep patting the rouged area with the puff so that no definite ending of the rouge will be apparent. In this way it will be blended into a nat-ural-looking blush. If after powdering the cheeks seem pale, add more rouge and repowder. For blond children use No. 18 rouge,[1] for brunettes use medium rouge, and for Negro chil-dren very dark rouge, and little of it. (Do not permit the skin to turn purple from over-rouging.) Now, when you have finished powdering and rouging, take your complexion brush and brush over the entire face, not forgetting the corners of the eyes.

CREPE HAIR

Hair can easily be applied as follows: hold the crepe hair in the left hand and with the right gently pull the loose end (Figs. 17 & 26a). You will notice that the hair unravels as the strings on which it is braided pull loose. Next, hold the hair about three inches from the unravelled part, and with a large-toothed comb comb off a few tufts of crepe hair. Remove this from the comb

[1] "No. 18 Rouge" is universally known under that designation.

in one mass, divide as needed, for moustache, beard, side-burns, etc. The hair in all cases should be used very sparingly, as it mats down and when dry appears darker. Before applying the hair, paint the face with spirit gum in the exact shape of the space you want hair to take (Figs. 26 & 26c). Allow this to dry a moment, then apply a second coat. While the first coat of spirit gum is drying separate the hair combed from the braid, and if it is to be used as a moustache, roll the hair lengthwise between the palms, cut off the desired length, twist the ends and curl them round a pencil, or else apply them straight on to the lips (Figs. 26 & 26j). For chin-whiskers or short beard pull the hair off the comb in the required width and length, separate one end a short way and stick the chin-whisker or goatee in place. The chin should be covered underneath as well as on top (Fig. 26c). For side-burns and whiskers comb the full length of crepe hair that has been pulled out, and from the temple-bone down to the chin, stick the hair in place. When you have reached the chin area duplicate the operation for the goatee or chin-whiskers, but use longer hair (Fig. 26c). The crepe hair is applied last, after the make-up is completed. To hold the hair in place use a cloth to press it down, and keep it there for a few seconds (Fig. 26g).

In pageants or school tableaux, the facial characteristics of the actors play an important part. For example, in portraying an historical picture where the characters are well known, such as *Custer's Last Stand,* get a picture of the situation wanted, and for Custer get a shoulder-length wig and apply the moustache, which droops down on each side of the mouth. This is sufficient to create the illusion. Of course, as you advance in the art of make-up you will require more detail in making the character.

CLOWNS

Clowns are roughly divided into three types, conventional, happy and sad. (Figs. 16a, b & c.) If a real skull-cap is not obtainable (this skull-cap is a hairless wig, generally white, entirely covering the hair), a good one can be made out of the top of a lady's white stocking, tying the part cut off with string and turning the stocking inside out; then cut two slits on each side for the ears to pass through. Clown white is applied evenly over face, neck and ears, so that no natural flesh color is visible. With a soft cloth wound round the index finger wipe off the areas you want colored, including the mouth, better known as clown lips. Paint these areas with the colors desired, powder well with white powder and retouch any colored area that needs brightening. Colors used are black, red, blue, green or combinations of these.

In connection with recitals or platform work, "characters" are done in the same way as for pageants and tableaux, but for straight make-up we divide the process, for convenience' sake, into two parts. Straight make-up is one that portrays an everyday, young to middle-aged man or woman.

STRAIGHT MAKE-UP, MALE

Apply a thin film of cold cream over the eyes and eyebrows; with the side of the point of the eyebrow pencil, darken the hairs of the eyebrows. Do not draw lines. Black pencil for dark hair, brown pencil for brown or titian or red hair, and light brown pencil for blondes. Eye-shadow may be used if desired, but use only a very slight touch of brown between the eyebrow and the upper eyelid, with the same pencil used for the eyebrows. Line the eyelids up close to the lashes and with a clean stump diffuse these lines so that a shaded edge is evident, not a hard line. If the little finger is used be sure not to enlarge these lines or smudge them: let the lines converge upon one common point at the orbital bone (see p. 23, also Figs. 26g, 42b, & d). With red liner touch the lips and rub the red into them so that they shall appear enlivened. Do not paint the lip; that is absolutely unnecessary. Do not rouge the cheeks, as this tends to make a man's face effeminate in appearance. If rouge is desired use medium rouge, rub up and down very lightly at the back of the cheeks in front of the ear, and let the length of the ears be your guide (see p. 23). Powder as follows: if male is blond, use light juvenile powder; red-head or brown, use flesh powder; brunette, use dark juvenile powder.

The above mentioned colors are made under different trade names by various manufacturers, but these are the basic colors obtainable anywhere. Finally, brush off the excess powder with the complexion brush.

STRAIGHT MAKE-UP, FEMALE

Apply a very thin film of cold cream to the eyebrows and eyelids; with the side of the point of the eyebrow pencil darken the upper half of the eyebrow. Do not draw lines (see p. 23).

EYE-SHADOW

If the woman is blonde use blue, blue-gray or violet eyeshadow. If red-head, titian or chestnut-haired, use green, dark or bright blue, brown or gray eye-shadow. If brunette, use green, violet or brown eye-shadow. There are gold and silver eye-shadows on the market, but there is no set rule for their use (see p. 23, Figs. 26g, 42b & d). Line the eyelids as close to the lashes as possible and diffuse the line with a stump or the little finger, so that there may be no evidence of a definite line (see p. 23, Figs. 42, b & d).

LIPS

The lips are then rouged. Care should be given to their shape; and note that cupid bows are no longer in style. The red liner may be used or, if preferred, moist or wet (liquid) rouge. The liner is applied direct to the lips which have previously been covered with a film of cold cream. Moist or cream rouge is applied with the little finger. Final shaping is done with the bevelled end of an orange stick (Fig. 41g). The lower lip is generally fuller. I am convinced that a generously proportioned pair of lips well executed denote character and lend greatly to the expression. If you can become adept at using a lip brush, which may be bought at most cosmetic departments, by all means do so. You will achieve a better-lasting surface.

ROUGE

Rouge for the cheeks comes next. Never rouge the hollows in cheeks. Rouge slightly *over* the hollow of the cheek. For a round or wide face rouge vertically closer to the nose. For a long face rouge farther back and more horizontally. Use a rabbit's foot (see p. 3, Fig. 11a). If the chin is long, rouge its base horizontally (see Figs. 12b & 11a). For blondes use No. 18 or orange rouge; lips should match if orange rouge is used. Red-heads, titians, chestnut-haired, use raspberry, strawberry or medium rouge. The lighter the hair the lighter the rouge. Brunettes use dark rouge. After the rouge is applied, powder the face from the forehead down. Blondes should use very light pink powder; red-heads, titians and chestnut-haired use naturelle or cream-color powder; brunettes use rachelle or light tan. When powdering the face keep patting the rouge on the cheeks until the color is completely blended, in order to produce a natural and healthy blush. Brush off the excess powder with the complexion brush. Of course, any untouched area such as neck, chest, back or arms are to be covered with the same-colored powder. Liquid powder, matching the skin color, is advised for neck, chest and arms. After applying with a soft sponge, rub the dried surface with the palm of the hand. This powder will not soil the clothing nearly so much as dry powder will.

EXERCISES

These must be done in front of a mirror with a good light on each side of the face. Use frosted electric light bulbs, fluorescent lights however, are best.

1. Pencil the eyebrows so that they are darkened according to instructions, not lined.

2. Line the lids so that the eyes appear shaded and framed, not lined.

3. Blend the eye shadow so that the eyes seem to sparkle.

4. Widen, lengthen or reshape the lips so that you can decide which form best brings out the character desired.

5. Rouge and powder the cheeks so that when you are finished you do not look "made up" from a reasonable distance—three to six feet.

A well-done straight make-up should not take longer than fifteen minutes.

When you have accomplished the above you are ready to advance to the more advanced courses. Remember, in the art and science of make-up it is necessary to practice. In that way alone can you become adept.

Crepe hair work is an art in itself and requires long practice. There are few people who really know how to handle crepe hair.

ADVANCED COURSE

GREASE PAINTS

Grease paints are manufactured in two forms, the commonly known stick, which comes in metal or cardboard tube containers, and the newer form, a creamy grease paint which comes in collapsible tubes or jars.

We must now learn all about grease paint sticks and liners, how to apply them, and why. There are various brands of grease paints, most of them good. Use the type you like best. Bear in mind that all cosmetics manufactured are controlled by the Pure Food and Drug Acts, the materials, essences and coloring matters are for the most part of the finest grades available.

Women, in particular, fear the growth of superfluous hair. However, the substances used in the manufacture of grease paints, I believe, will not cause the growth of hair. It is generally known that actors have good skins even after many years' use of grease paints. Grease paints are carefully compounded and can be placed in the same category with skin conditioners.

Grease paint sticks come in various shades (see p. 33). Buy the colors you need and add to these as you need more. For example, you are cast in the role of an old man, bald, very gray and eccentric. For this you would need the following colors: one stick sallow old man grease paint, one stick yellow liner for highlighting (if you prefer very pale flesh you may use that instead of yellow), one stick medium brown liner for wrinkles, one stick dark maroon liner for accentuating wrinkles and shadows, one stick white liner for graying eyebrows and also for highlighting, one stick dark gray liner for shading the parts appearing as unshaven, one

21

small box of black wax for blocking out the teeth (if missing teeth are called for), one container of nose putty for altering the shape of the nose, making moles, or for prominent brows, one bundle of stumps for blending the make-up lines or shadows, 12 inches of light gray crepe hair, and a bottle of spirit gum. Buy the powder in the same shades as the grease paint (some manufacturers urge a lighter shade powder, but this is optional), a few powder puffs and a complexion brush. So far, everything you will have bought may be used again for similar characters, the only addition necessary being the color of other grease paints and powder for other roles. Of course, different shades of hair must be used for different characters.

Grease paint is also sold in collapsible tubes. The substance is a cream instead of a molded stick, and every skin shade is distinguished by a number. For instance, if you want sallow old man and you know the colors by number you would order No. 6, which is sallow. If you don't know what number the color is, you should simply order Sallow.

The liners are made in moist or pomade form; if you want yellow you order No. 11 liner. What I have just said has to do with grease paint; the same thing applies to liner colors. The technique for application is different from that of grease paint sticks. We are now ready to take up the technique of the application of grease paint.

GREASE PAINT STICK TECHNIQUE

Males. Cover the face, neck and ears with a light film of cold cream. Use very sparingly; if too much cold cream is used the make-up will be greasy and messy and cause profuse perspiration. Push the grease paint (with the finger) up out of the tube from the bottom, so that the cap rises with it about half an inch from the top of the tube. Remove the cover and with the flat end at the top cover the forehead, eyelids, cheeks, sides and front of the nose, the area around the lips and chin with the flesh color selected. With the palms of the hands spread the color evenly over the face, neck and ears so that the entire skin area exposed is smoothly and evenly covered.

Next, take the proper shade (black if brunette, brown if blond) of eyebrow pencil and darken the eyebrows and line the eyelids. Diffuse the lid lines with the finger or stump. Use very light brown eye shadow, and no rouge. Yet, if rouge must be used apply dry rouge with the rabbit's foot behind the cheek, in front of the ear, the length of the ear being your guide. Lips should be very lightly touched up or wiped off. If thicker lips are required, use dark maroon and apply carefully. Be sure not to make a cupid's bow on the upper lip. Apply the powder in the proper shade, from the forehead down all over the face, neck and ears, and brush off the excess with the complexion brush. This is called *straight* make-up, which includes heroes, historical or romantic, juvenile and chorus, in fact, almost any type of young or middle-aged man with a clean-shaven face.

Female. For female make-up proceed as above described, using light flesh or natural grease paint. Next, line the eyebrows carefully, being sure to arch the brow and run the pencil down on the temple (Fig. 26g). Long experience and many experiments convince me that a longer eyebrow in most cases "frames" the eye and gives it glamor. This line must be soft and follow the contour of the upper eyelid. As the line is continued, it may be drawn straight across, slightly lowered in the direction of the top of the ears, or with a slightly perceptible dip as in Figs. 42b & d. Select the eye shadow, as explained on p. 18, and apply it with the little finger and shade as shown in Fig. 42d. You line the lids next according to the type of eye you wish to suggest. Blend these lines smoothly with the stump. Then apply the lip rouge. (Fig. 41) You are now ready to rouge the cheeks. Figs. 11a, b & c will show how to select your type face, and rouge accordingly. Powder the face well. The lip rouge will be "set" by smartly patting the lips with powder. This absorbs excess moisture or grease and allows the lips to remain made up throughout any performance. After removing excess powder with your complexion brush, moisten the lips and mascara the eyelashes. If the neck and shoulders are in evidence use liquid powder of the same shade as your face foundation color, or powder the visible areas. Hands and arms are very important. They are too often neglected. Don't forget them.

CREPE HAIR

The subject of crepe hair is extensive. You already know that crepe hair comes in tight braids and can be pulled out for manipulation and used as shown in Figs. 17 & 26a. However, in this course I shall explain the more advanced technique. Whatever role you wish to play you should look life-like and the hair should appear to be "growing out of the skin," and not stuck on. Hair has character just like any other part of the human anatomy. Hair is divided into four classes: woolly or fuzzy, wavy, straight, cut-crepe hair.

1. Woolly or fuzzy hair is often used for Negro types, insane and derelict characters.

2. Wavy hair is used for old characters, Biblical characters, outdoor types, etc.

3. Straight hair is used for any character where a natural growth of hair is to be depicted—also Chinese, Japanese and Mongolian types.

4. Cut-crepe hair is used for natural unshaven effects. The technique of applying woolly or fuzzy crepe hair is as follows: pull out the crepe hair from the braid, the length being less than is actually used because of the stretching properties of the hair. After the hair is pulled out to the desired length cut it off as shown in Fig. 26a. The hair is then divided into parts for eyebrows, moustache, beard, etc. It may be pulled apart with the fingers; this leaves a natural-looking "edge" for sticking on to the face. If it is not pulled apart it may be trimmed with scissors. The "pulled" method will give the appearance of hair growing out naturally because hair where it begins to grow, next to the bare skin, must be almost invisible to the eye. If the "trimmed" method is used the hair must be thinned along the border, where it is stuck on to the face.

If the effect of wavy hair is desired, proceed as shown in Fig. 17.

After the hair is cut from the braid put a damp cloth over the hair and iron it out, carefully stretching it while damp; then press again. The application to the face is as shown in Figs. 26-a to j. See also Fig. 43.

To make crepe hair straight, wet a cloth, such as an ironing-cloth, but do not wring it out dry. Place the already cut and pulled crepe hair on another damp cloth and press with a hot iron until the cloth is dry. Pull the crepe hair between the hands carefully, so as to straighten but not separate the strands, and repeat until the hair is absolutely straight. See photograph of Mandarin (Fig. 32). The ironing out of crepe hair, in all cases, is done with one "pulled section" at a time.

Cut-crepe hair is used for unshaven effects. Figs. 17c, 18, 19. After the hair is ironed, cut the straight hair into bits no longer than $\frac{1}{16}$ of an inch each; paint the area you wish covered very sparingly with spirit gum. With a rough towel wound round the fingers, pick up the cut hair and carefully and evenly daub it on. This must be done with special care. Remember, this process doesn't require much hair, because, to appear natural, the skin must "peek through." Figs. 18 & 19.

After the hair has been pulled out, fasten the end cut from the unbraided portion, right up to where it was pulled out, to some stationary object on a table, or by tying it. Take the extreme end, nearest you, between the fingers of the left hand and with the right thumb and first and second fingers carefully run your right hand across the pulled-out section until the hair is fluffy and stands out, so that the strands are seen as practically separated from each other. Fig. 17.

In applying straight crepe hair, fasten it to the lowest part of the face and build it upward. *Shingle* the hair, placing the additional hairs to one side or over the first layer, as in shingling a roof. Fig. 17a. When the spirit gum is dry the hair may be combed and trimmed to any desired shape. Moustaches are applied the same way. If, after this hair is stuck in place, it is too straight, moisten the ends of the moustache with water and curl around a pencil, then carefully comb until the proper curve or curl is secured. The ends of the moustache may be waxed, curled, or turned up or down by sticking down the middle part of the end to the upper lip, the tip ends being left free. Notice how hair grows, following the contour of the face; short eyebrows grow across, long eyebrows grow down, beards grow down, and also moustaches.

In applying eyebrows for old-age types, apply the spirit gum above and cover the brow Figs. 25a & 26i, and let the crepe hair fall down and over the natural eyebrow.

BLOCKING OUT EYEBROWS

There are three proper ways to block out eyebrows:
1. Soaping out.
2. Blocking out with grease paint.
3. Masking.

1. **Soaping out.** Moisten a cake of white soap slightly. Rub the cake back and forth so that the soap gets under the hair as well as over it. Finally, with an upward motion, finish flattening the eyebrow against the frontal bones. Cover with foundation grease paint as used on the face; powder, then either draw on, or apply crepe hair eyebrows in the proper shape.

2. **Blocking out with grease paint.** This is done with a stick of grease paint of a lighter shade than that used for the foundation of the face. Rub the flat end of the stick as explained for "soaping out." Then take the same foundation color and flatten the hairs upward toward the forehead, using a pressing and rotating motion rather than rubbing or spreading; powder, then apply the crepe hair brow as desired. By dipping the end of the eyebrow pencil very lightly in cold cream, the new eyebrow may be easily pencilled on.

3. **Masking.** In making my reconstruction of the Neanderthal Man, Figs. 47 & 48, I found that very prominent frontals were vitally important, for two reasons. First, to give

the appearance of the receding brow and to follow in detail the results of my research, which in every case depicted a very prominent bifurcated brow. Therefore I masked the eyebrows as follows: one-inch surgical bandage was trimmed to cover the length and breadth of the eyebrows. (Fig. 33a) This was stuck down to the skin all round the edges, with flexible collodion. The proper amount of nose putty was kneaded into a thin wide shell to cover the bandage; then with the fingers the nose putty was blended so that the edges of the putty were invisible, even to the eye of the camera. After the shell is applied, nose putty is moulded into any shape desired. The most surprising effects can be obtained, because there is no fear of the putty bubbling or getting loose, and removal is very easy. Of course, before applying the hair eyebrow, the putty and face is covered with the color grease paint selected, properly powdered, and then brushed off with the complexion brush. Fig. 33a.

For masking out moustaches the same method is used, and the mouth and lips are always easily movable. Fig. 17b. For added assurance spirit gum is painted over the gauze about a quarter of an inch wide, so that the putty will not bubble. See Fig. 17b.

Following are the skin colors for old people: 1. Healthy, 2. Ruddy, 3. Outdoor, 4. Indoor, 5. Eccentric.

"Healthy," "Ruddy," etc., are recognized names given to the flesh colors of grease paints. Numbers 1, 2, 3, are more or less alike, the only difference being in skin color and neatness of hair and dress. Number 1 may also be any one of the three. Number 2 includes army officers, naval officers, athletic executives, retired wealthy types, mechanics, magnates, industrialists, leaders, etc. Fig. 26j would cover the following types; backwoodsman,[1] policeman, letter-carriers, officers, detectives, laborers, tramps, fishermen, etc. Figs. 26ja to jd, include misers, bookworms, judges, Biblical characters, sickly

---

[1] Please note that in referring to various types of persons I use such words as "mechanics," "leaders," etc. only in the broadest sense. To do this without making qualifications is merely a convenience; it simplifies my explanation.

ailing types, professors, inventors, religious, etc. Figs. j, jb
& jd cover eccentric characters.

MALE, OLD AGE

When an "old" character is made up the color of grease paint
is chosen in conformity with the age and type of the character.
After the foundation is applied, turn your attention to the
mouth. Should the script call for a very old character, erase the
lips entirely with foundation color, highlight and line the mouth
as in Fig. 41e. Next make up the eyes. The prominence of
wrinkles, pouches, and sunken orbits also depends on the character and age. After the eyes and mouth are made up the nose
is altered as desired and wrinkled and shaded according to
character. Fig. 35b. Next comes the forehead. If a blend wig is
used, grease paint the forehead first, higher than the front edge
of the wig, and then put the wig on, being sure the blender
(front part) fits snugly. If a tighter wig is needed the wig may
be "pleated" on each side behind the ears, pleated on the inside
with a few stitches, or even pinned. Another method is to tape
down the blend (the front of the wig, over the forehead) with
a one-inch strip of adhesive tape, being sure that it is long
enough to span the forehead, yet not long enough to engage the
hair at the temples. This is all covered over smoothly with
grease paint, and the wig-line hidden from view by the addition of wrinkles on the forehead, leaving the blend line to simulate one wrinkle. The painted wrinkles being made, over and
below with brown or maroon liner and highlighted. Figs. 27,
35 & 49.

Next the cheeks. Follow the skeletal structure of the jaw and
cheek-bone so that the hollows will appear absolutely natural.
If an unshaven effect is desired this may be secured with cut-
crepe hair, as described on page 25. Satisfactory results may
also be obtained by using gray liner rubbed on the skin, jaws
and upper lip to show stubble.

If the character is pale, wan or waxen in appearance use light

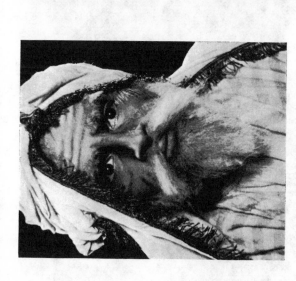

FIG. 13. BEDOUIN SHEIK

A young man 20 years of age made up by the Author.

FIG. 14. EDWARD EVERETT HALE

CARL KREBS *in the Author's make-up.*

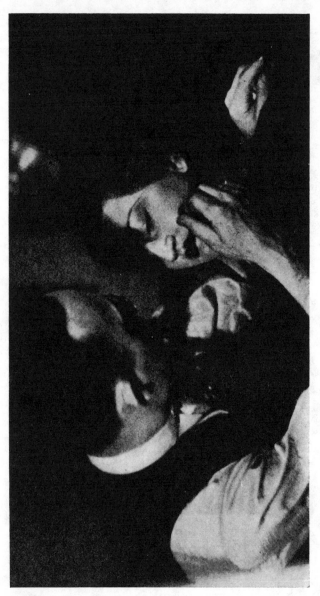

FIG. 15. *The Author shows position when making up a subject. Always work AWAY from the center of the face.*

16

EYEBROWS AND LIPS SAME COLOR

ALL DIAMONDS SAME COLOR

BLACK VERTICAL EYE LINES AND SMILE LINES

16a

16b

CONVENTIONAL CLOWN

SAD CLOWN.

IN ALL OF THE ABOVE, NOTICE HOW ENLARGED MOUTH IS MADE OVER NATURAL MOUTH.

HAPPY CLOWN.

CLOWN WIGS ARE AVAILABLE WITH HAIR IN BRIGHT COLORS. COLORED CREPE HAIR CAN BE USED FOR BEARDS ETC.

16c

PIERROT (SAD).
THERE IS ALSO THE HAPPY PIERROT

FIG. 16. *The natural lips are shown thru the made up lips to give exact shape of the mouth make-up.*

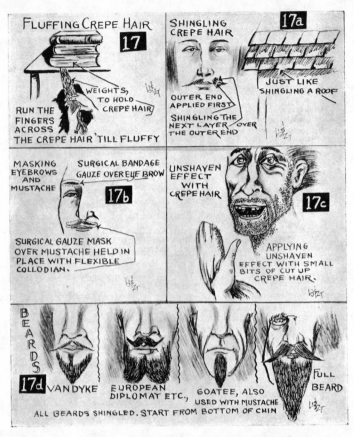

FIG. 17. *On the screen, artificial beards and mustaches photograph more naturally than real hair.*

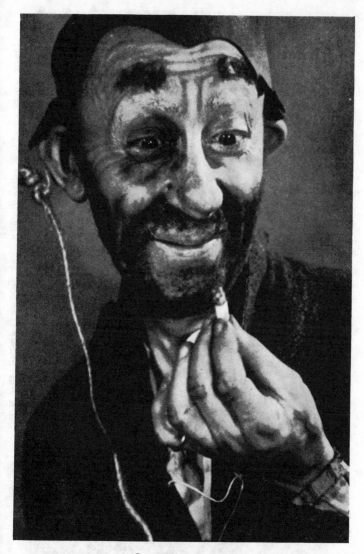

FIG. 18. BURLESQUE TRAMP

The Author in his laugh provoking make-up.

Note: Eyebrows, mustache blocked out, putty nose and "cut" crepe hair.

FIG. 19. *Profile of the Burlesque Tramp, showing nose structure and upper lip construction.*

FIG. 20. MISS HELEN B. LISZT
In the Author's make-up as a Mammy.

gray liner; for healthier types use darker gray, powder well, apply hair as desired, and mascara eyelashes in white.

FEMALE, OLD AGE

In female characters follow the same rules as for the males, only do not use false eyebrows. Mascara the eyebrows and eyelashes in white. If moles are called for, make them of nose putty, apply to the skin, which is wiped free of grease paint and cold cream; then press the edges down with the bevelled edge of the orange stick.

EXERCISES

1. Cover the face with grease paint so smoothly that you can see your own pores. It should be evenly covered with foundation color.

2. Use the stump, as explained, in order that you may handle it at all angles rapidly without fear of jabbing your eye.

3. Use the tip of the finger for blending until you can blend the line with ease, not wipe it off or smudge it.

4. Practice making lips so that you can duplicate the same style more than once without difficulty.

5. Rouge the cheeks so that you cannot detect where the rouge ends.

6. Practice various forms, shapes and types of beards, moustaches, eyebrows. This exercise can hardly be repeated too often. Learn how to handle crepe hair deftly, effectively.

7. Grease paint out the eyebrows; you will find this method a quick one. Practice brushing up and blocking out.

8. Practice wrinkling and blending, using both the stump and little finger. In order to be efficient you must keep practicing.

Learn all you can by practice and when you have mastered this course you are ready for the Special Advanced course instruction.

SPECIAL ADVANCED COURSE

This chapter outlines the technique of using grease paint that comes in collapsible tubes or jars. "Cream" grease paint is made of the finest materials. This product is made by various manufacturers in the following foundations or complexion colors: white, flesh, peach, light juvenile, dark juvenile, sunburn (ruddy), Indian, carmine, cream, rachelle, sallow, olive, suntan, Oriental, Hawaiian (Hindu), Mulatto (Negro), black.[1]

Eye shadow and lining colors to match the above-mentioned foundation grease paints are made of a slightly more solid base. This form of eye shadow is sold in tins. The colors are used both as liners and as eye shadows. The colors are white, light blue, dark blue, blue-green, blue-gray, gray, light brown, dark brown, green, lavender, carmine, crimson, black.

MAKING UP WITH CREAM GREASE PAINT

Prepare the face by applying a thin film of cold cream all over the exposed area of the face, neck, ears, and behind the ears as well. Bear in mind that a greasy face (too much cold cream) is hard to make up and will appear smudgy. It is also easily smeared. Use only enough to cover thinly the areas which are to receive the foundation color. Modern formulas have improved to the point where cold cream is unnecessary in the application of tube foundation color if one cares to omit its application.

[1] As in stick grease paint, the flesh colors "olive," "sunburn," etc. are indicated by a number. If ordered by color there is less danger of getting the wrong shade. Different manufacturers number the same color differently.

FOUNDATION TECHNIQUE

In the palm of the left hand squeeze about a quarter of an inch of the foundation color desired. Moisten the fingers of the right hand and dab the grease paint all over the face. When the face is completely covered with foundation grease paint, dip the hands in water and spread the foundation color evenly and smoothly all over the covered area. Use both hands in spreading the foundation color all over the exposed area. Complexions that are clear need less foundation color than ruddy complexions. Whenever another color is to be used, omit the foundation color. Finally, pat the face with the moist fingers to give the make-up a dull, uniform and smooth appearance.

LINING WITH POMADE LINING COLORS

Stump Technique. Lines on the face are made by dipping the stump into the color selected and drawn lightly across the surface to be lined. Rotate the stump between thumb and forefinger very slowly as the line is being drawn. Never *dig* the stump into the lining color; turn it slowly on the surface. After the line is drawn, soften with the little finger, going over the lines already "stumped."

Brush Technique. If the brush technique is used, add a few drops of water to the lining color, and with a finely pointed sable brush (which may be bought at any art supply store) draw the lines needed. When making wrinkles, the dark lines are indicated with a pointed brush. Highlighting is done with a wider (about ¼-inch) short-haired sable brush. The brush must be soft, yet of a good resilient quality so that the hairs spring back to their original position. A good way to test a brush for make-up purposes is to wet it between the lips and press it down on the thumbnail; if the hairs lie down when wet, don't use it. The ¼-inch brush is also used for eye-shadowing. Keep the brush moist with water, in order to *fade* the areas and edges needed for blending.

LIPS

Lips are first outlined with the pointed brush, then filled in with the wider brush.

EYEBROWS

Eyebrows are made with the pointed brush.

ROUGE

Rouging is better done with the rabbit's foot if cake (dry) rouge is used, but a good rule is to apply first an "under rouge" of a slightly lighter color. This rouge is moist or cream rouge and is applied with the fingers. When the face is powdered and brushed off, re-rouge with a dry rouge slightly darker in color, using the rabbit's foot; then re-powder again.

There is a make-up known as *Water Moist*. This is produced as a "greaseless make-up" with no need of cold cream as a base, and no call for powder to finish the make-up. The method of make-up is just the same as for tube grease paint, but starting with the foundation or skin color desired. The technique is the same, using moist fingers and the palms for even distribution of color. Instead of rouge use any one of the red colors mentioned below and work the color into the cheeks as is done with rouge.

For removal of *Water Moist* use only soap and water, but plenty of it. *Water Moist* is also recommended as a liquid paint. Dissolve the contents of the tube in water and apply the color to the arms, legs, chest, etc. with a silk sponge (which may be had at any drug store), or a 1-inch brush (which may be had at any hardware store), then smooth all over with moist fingers in order to even the foundation where applied.

Water Moist comes in the following foundation colors:

Pale flesh	Natural	Dark juvenile
Light flesh	Light juvenile	Light sunburn

Dark sunburn
Sallow young
  man
Healthy middle
  age
Sallow old man
Ruddy old man
Light olive
Dark olive
Gipsy
Moor
Ultramarine blue
Navy blue
Chinese
Indian
East Indian
Japanese

Mulatto
White
Black
* Light carmine
* Dark carmine
Canary yellow
Golden yellow
Orange yellow
Yellowish flesh
Purplish flesh
Hawaiian
Yellowish
  brown
Green
Dark Hawaiian
Dark yellow
West Indian

Blond
Brunette
* Light crimson
* Dark crimson
Light gray
Dark gray
Lavender
Light brown
Dark brown
Sky blue
Robin's egg
  blue
Turquoise blue
Light cobalt
  blue
Dark cobalt
  blue

The colors indicated by asterisks can be applied as rouge to the cheeks. These are mentioned in the previous chapter, page 19.

A personal hint. In applying "Water Moist" I advise the utmost care and sparseness in its application, because it dries chalky if used too thickly.

Personally, I prefer grease paints, but the student may find novel and good effects with "water moistened" paint, if it is used with due caution.

Tube grease paint make-up will now be taken up.

Theatrical cosmetic manufacturers have developed an even skin-covering grease paint that is uniform in texture and color. After using every kind of make-up material, I recommend Theatrical Advanced tube or jar grease paints, because the colors are basically the same, and no matter where you buy a certain color grease paint you will find it right.

In this course we deal only with special grease paints, liners and powders.

You may always order these grease paints by the foundation

color name. As previously stated it is safer to order grease paint by skin color such as "Arab," "Juvenile," etc., since no two manufacturers number these colors alike.

The colors by which the skin foundations are known are given here in all their varieties.

They come in collapsible tubes and jars of uniform quality and colors.

TUBE OR JAR GREASE PAINTS

Very light pink	Light cream	Spanish	Mikado
Light juvenile	Special cream	Dark sunburn	Light lavender
Light pink	Yellow	Mexican	Lavender
Pink	Olive	East Indian	White
Juvenile	Orange	Arab	Light Negro
Flesh	Sallow	Indian	Dark Negro
Flesh, juvenile	Tan	Mulatto	Red

LINING PASTE COLORS IN TINS

Black	Blue gray	Medium blue
Dark brown	Blue green	White
Light brown	Lavender-purple	Purple-bronze
Dark blue	Maroon crimson	Bronze
Light blue	Green	Gray
	Special blue	

THEATRICAL SPECIAL ADVANCED MAKE-UP TECHNIQUE

Women should remove all street make-up, wiping the face clean. Men should be fresh-shaved. No cold cream is necessary. Squeeze about ¼-inch of grease paint from the tube into the palm of the left hand. With the fingers of the right hand spot the face with the foundation color until it is well covered. Spread these spots until they merge into one smooth covering all over the exposed area you want covered. Then remove all grease paint from the hands, dip them in water and while moist, smooth the grease paint evenly and thinly all over the covered areas. Be sure that the fingers are moist, even if it takes redipping into the water until the foundation is distributed completely and the finished color is smooth and even. Finally, dip your hands into water again and carefully pat the face all over making the entire surface as smooth as possible.

The eye-shadow is applied with the little finger as explained on pages 2, 18.

The eyebrow pencil is applied after the eye-shadow. This is also explained on pages 8, 14.

Moist rouge, called under-rouge, is then applied.

The brush is used again for shaping the lips.

The above-described order is advised in using make-up so that there will be no smudging, and the made-up present a neat appearance.

Next, with a wool powder puff, powder all over the make-up areas so that all shine is toned down, and the blending is smooth and even.

I urge applying the dry rouge next, and toning it carefully with the powder puff. When this is done, apply mascara to the eyelashes.

Artificial eyelashes are available in all natural colors, Fig. 8, also blue, green, etc. They are applied with a specific adhesive substance that comes with the eyelash outfit. Spirit gum should be used with caution: it irritates the eyes. Eyelashes are easily removed, but it requires deftness to apply them so that they look natural and do not interfere with the movements of the eye and cause discomfort.

Theatrical Advanced make-up powders are made to match the make-up. I give them here:

White	Light cream
Light pink	Cream
Pink	Light lavender
Ruddy	Lavender
Healthy tan	Medium brown
Naturelle	Spanish
Rachelle	Special light cream
Outdoor, neutral	Indian
Sunburn	Hindu
Flesh	Othello

If any particular color of powder is desired, it is not difficult to combine two or more shades. For instance, cream color mixed with sunburn color powder will produce a healthy colored powder, not as "hot" as sunburn, yet warm and glowing.

Mixing is done in a separate jar or tin with a tight cover. Put some sunburn powder in the container, add cream powder, cover tight and shake well until the colors are blended. You will soon learn to tell when the color is of the desired hue.

For the removal of this make-up apply cold cream. It is important to rub the cream all over the made-up areas until the foundation is "loosened." Do not rub *in*. A soft steady rotating motion is most effective, then with a cloth or cleansing tissue, wipe off the make-up. Do not bear down on the skin when taking make-up off. It is not necessary to exert pressure.

After the face is profusely powdered and carefully and completely brushed off, apply spirit gum as explained on page 25. For the removal of crepe hair, first pull off all the hair that can be separated from the face. This is easily and quickly done. Next, apply a generous amount of cold cream to this area and **with** a steady rotating motion, covering only one area at a time,

FIG. 21. The Author studying John D. Rockefeller, Sr.'s portrait in preparation for making up his own face as the famous financier.

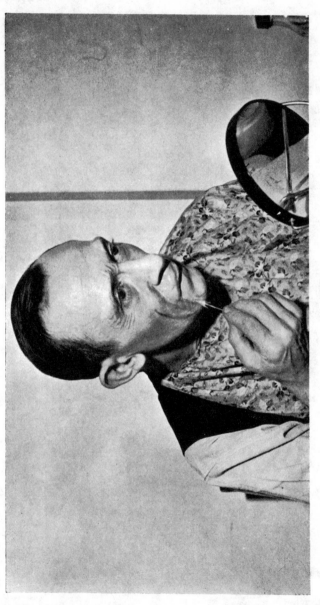

FIG. 22. *Foundation grease paint has been applied. Eyebrows and mustache are blocked out according to the instructions given. Lining of "crows feet" is shown.*

FIG. 23. *Note the "furrows", the "pouches under the eyes" and hollowed cheeks. Age lines are started around mouth and on chin.*

FIG. 24. *The Author's final characterization of John D. Rockefeller, Sr. This set of pictures is from a series by the Author appearing in "Pic." (By courtesy of "Pic.")*

steadily rub the crepe hair still on the face, and it will come off the skin in the form of small wads or balls. This is the easiest and most convenient method. However, should stubborn bits of hair remain around the eyebrows or where any stubble of beard has not been cleanly shaved, alcohol will finish the process. Acetone, U.S.P., for sale in almost any drug store is a safe and quick remover. Keep away from the eyes or broken skin areas.

If nose putty is to be removed take the bulk of the putty with the fingers. Roll this into a ball and with quick dabs, use the removed portion to take off as much as will stick to it. What is left is softened with cold cream and easily wiped off.

There is also a liquid make-up for arms, legs, shoulders, chest and back which matches every color of grease paint. It is applied with a stroke motion in one direction, until it is perfectly dry. It is easily removed with soap and water.

TESTING MAKE-UP FOR DISTANCE

A good way to test your make-up for distance is to stand before a *large* mirror. Then with a small mirror (say 11 × 14 inches) held in front of you, facing the larger mirror; you will get a multiple arrangement of mirrors, each reflection further away from you than the one in front of it. Thus you can see yourself at a great distance. A few moments' experimenting will give you the proper angle and height. Bear in mind that electric light bulbs must be facing you, arranged at the sides of the larger mirror facing you, as in the original arrangement of the make-up mirror.

CHARACTER MAKE-UP

Next come the various "Character" make-ups. There will be no mention of the method of make-up, because by now you should be familiar with that subject. The present chapter helps the student complete the "creation" of a character, whether with the use of stick grease paint or tubes. By now the student should know how to apply the specific medium he intends to use, also how to apply wrinkles, shadows, hair, and to characterize youth, middle or old age. Keep in mind that although certain characters have been seen portrayed on the stage or screen for many years, if these characters are fictional, you are allowed the latitude of adding or altering, by make-up, almost any feature you like. For example, one famous tragedian portrayed Cyrano de Bergerac without any chin-whisker but with a generous flowing moustache.

I start with a few of the Shakespearean roles. If you want a special character make-up, one not mentioned here, go to the library, get a photograph or illustration, or even a printed description of the character, and try to reproduce it or improve on it. Use your imagination. This can be a very valuable kind of exercise.

Only some of the typical characters are given here where specific make-up is most essential.

HAMLET: "Straight," no rouge. Lips pale, brown eye shadow (deep). Brown hair, wavy pompadour style.

POLONIUS: "Old age" Figs. 35, a, b. Bald, white shoulder-length wig. White moustache and beard. Beard at temple joining wig should be light gray, blended with the white, lower down on face.

THE GHOST: A shroud is used and should be of such color as to appear blended with the color of the background.

For foundation use yellow. Shade each side of nose down to nostrils, making the nose appear thin and long. Highlight the bridge of the nose and blend with white. Eyebrows are lined in black, Fig. 42e. Shading is warm brown all around, Fig. 25e. The cheeks are deeply hollowed in warm brown. Fig. 35a. Very light gray crepe hair ironed out almost straight. Long drooping moustache and full but pointed beard, Fig. 17d. Highlight cheek-bones, brow over eyebrows, and have the beard "grow out" on the cheeks *under* the cheek-bones. Beard should be trimmed. The effect sought should be deep-set eyes, pale wan face, and sad eyebrows. No wrinkles.

QUEEN OF DENMARK: "Straight," past middle age.

CLOWNS: 1st Grave-digger: Fat, jolly. Ruddy foundation.

Big red lips, red nose and cheeks. Thick eyebrows. Red or chestnut wig.

2nd Grave-digger: Thin, small; pale foundation. Eyes, see Fig. 25e. Thick lower lip.

Captain: Healthy old-age foundation. No moustache. Thick lower lip; erase upper lip with foundation. Curly crepe hair beard under chin and around jaw up to front of ears on temples. Thick eyebrows, Fig. 42a.

For making-up old age lines see Figs. 35, a, b & c.

Julius Cæsar: Titian-colored partly bald wig. Ruddy complexion, hollowed cheeks, deep-set eyes, cleft chin and determined jaw.

Mark Antony: "Straight," robust, dynamic, red hair.

Soothsayer and Artemictorus: Old, bald, full moustache and beard.

Othello: Dark, Moor foundation but *no* negroid features. Small moustache and pointed beard (about 2 inches long).

Iago: A small villainous type. Moustache and beard, Fig. 17d. Sallow young man grease paint, deep lines from sides of nostrils down on each side of mouth.

King Lear: Regal character. Eyes, see Fig. 25d. Ruddy old man foundation. For lining and shading, see Figs. 25c, 35, a, & 42c. White wig, white full beard and moustache.

Note: The clowns in Shakespeare usually take Jester make-up; long chins, hooked noses, thin mouths turned up at corners. For eyebrows see Fig. 25f. They also have ruddy complexions, red noses and cheeks.

Macbeth: Sandy, gray shoulder-length wig, slightly darker moustache, drooping and flowing beard, but not too thick. Sallow complexion, high cheek-bones. For nose, see Fig. 36. Eyes, see Fig. 25e. Eyebrows, see Fig. 25d.

Shylock: See Fig. 43.

Light gray bald wig, with or without forelock, shoulderlength. Eyes, Figs. 25a, 26j & 42a. Nose, Figs. 36 & 54. For lining see Figs. 35, a & b. Sallow old man foundation. Lines and shadows in warm brown. Very light gray, slightly curly moustache and beard. Block out one or two front upper teeth. For hand see Fig. 43.

FALSTAFF: Sunburn base. For face contour see Fig. 55b. Round tipped nose. Gray hair and beard.

Of course, there are complicated make-ups where "tricks" are used in order to complete the illusion. These will be discussed later on.

Stage types, historical characters, fictional characters and burlesque make-up will now be discussed.

INDIAN: NORTH AMERICAN

Study the type under consideration. There are any number of good plates available in libraries. In most characters coming under the heading of "native types" the males are made-up with darker skins than the females.

Grease foundation: Indian (well covered for males), nose, high bridge, aquiline. Add high cheek-bones (see page 64). Full lips and well-defined chin and jaw-bones. Shading and lining (males only). Shadow in dark brown under cheek-bones. Shadow under lower lip, yet over the chin to make chin prominent. Deep lines drawn on each side of mouth from the nostrils. War paint (when called for) is added with the following colors: red, bright blue, white or yellow. The markings may be circles, crosses, triangles, parallel lines as the case may be, and are applied to forehead, cheeks, nose and chin. First wipe off the foundation color in the design or form to be colored, then apply the colors as desired over the wiped-off area. If a red circle is to be applied, wipe a circle from the face; a clean red circle can then be applied in the same place. Powder well *before* applying these facial designs. For other exposed parts of the body use liquid make-up, which is applied with a soft sponge and rubbed carefully until dry. It will not come off until washed off with soap and water.

NEGRO

Negro make-up is of two types, minstrel or burlesque, and natural. Minstrel make-up is simple. Burnt cork or black grease paint is used, covering the entire exposed area of the face, neck and ears. For the mouth see Fig. 41d. The corners of the mouth may be made to turn up or down as desired. Do not paint the mouth red, leave it natural or paint the lip area with flesh grease paint. Black or white gloves are needed where the hands are not made up. The tops of a pair of men's black hose can be used on the wrists; white wrists should not, of course, be visible. A curly wig completes the make-up. For the natural Negro type, Othello, Negro, or Moor grease paint is used. This foundation is evenly applied to the exposed areas. The eyebrows are blackened and wrinkles or shadows are done in black, and should be well blended. The lips are enlarged by a very dark maroon liner. The backs of the hands are made up but the palms are not. Note Fig. 20. This is a young miss of sixteen, yet made up to represent the good-natured type of conventional mammy.

CHINESE AND JAPANESE TYPES

The chief differences between Chinese and Japanese facial make-up are as follows:

1. Chinese eyes slant more.

2. Japanese hair is sparser.

3. Chinese moustaches droop and are long. (I.e., the old time conventional types. Nowadays the style is different.)

4. Japanese moustaches are bristle-like, stand out, and are nearly always short. If beards are used they are also short, never over one and a half inches wide.

5. Japanese lips and noses are often thinner.

6. Chinese heads are half bald, where queues are used. (Again, this refers to older and more conventional types.)

For Japanese eyes see Fig. 42f.

For Chinese eyes see Figs. 25b, 32, 42c.

7. Chinese (classic or older types) have long finger nails, especially on the little finger. Fig. 32 & 56b. Japanese do not.

8. Japanese wigs (not mentioning the stereotyped operatic characters) are straight-haired and full wigs, mostly short

cropped pompadours. Only the very old characters are bald.

For Chinese Mandarin see Fig. 32. For Chinese nails see Figs. 32 & 56b.

9. Foundation of the specific color should be used. Do not use olive or any other yellow color. There is a specific "Chinese" or "Oriental" grease paint. Never use rouge on an Oriental male character.

10. Female Japanese are rouged directly in the center of the cheeks just below each eye and not too well blended.

11. Be sure and make a very small but well defined cupid's bow mouth. Chinese women's lips are fuller. Chinese women's hair is not like the high combed hair of Geisha girls. Simple. Parted in the center with a low "bun" at the nape of the neck. Note: The nose of the Chinese should be made as in Figs. 32, 36a & 54a.

HAG OR WITCH

Fig. 50

This character is made up according to the period, the story and the type called for in the play used. Foundation, use yellowish flesh, sallow young man or yellow. Build up a high-bridged nose. (Figs. 36 & 54.) Add eyebrows as Figs. 26j, 25a & 42a. Wrinkle forehead as in Fig. 35. Cover the upper lip entirely with foundation grease paint. Line and shade the eyes as in Figs. 25a & 42a, and line the mouth as in Figs. 35c & 41e, but turn the corners of the mouth down. Shade and line the cheeks as in Fig. 35a. Be sure to highlight each line and shadow carefully and sharply, in order to bring out the crispness of the make-up. Block out two or three teeth, see Fig. 56a, leaving a tooth visible between those blocked out. A long straggly wig finishes the make-up. Do not forget the hands, old, thin, knotty and long nails. See Fig. 43.

MEPHISTO OR DEVIL

Figs. 44 & 45

This type can be made up with flesh foundation, with reddened nose and cheeks, or entirely in red grease paint. For eyes and eyebrows see Fig. 25. The eyebrows may be either painted on or made with crepe hair. Make nose as in Figs. 36 & 54. If natural grease paint is used, lining is done in warm browns and strengthened with the stump in red liner. Wrinkles and deep furrows are lined in between the eyebrows, Figs. 25 & 45, vertically and strongly highlighted. The moustache is then applied, slanting up on each side of the lip, the ends pointed and twisted. A thin, pointed chin goatee is then applied. The eyes should be deeply shaded in dark red or very warm brown, and the cheekbones highlighted and *under-shadowed* to make them prominent. Two deep lines from the nostrils on each side of the mouth, well highlighted, will help accentuate the mouth, which should be made full-lipped, with corners turned up. (The head-dress of the costume may have two horns or a pointed cap with a straight feather.)

BEDOUIN SHEIK, FAKIR, HINDU

Fig. 13

The Turk, Hindu, Arab and East Indian are similar in color. Sallow, lean of flesh, prominent nose, determined chin, well-defined brows, and cheek-bones. It is in the "untouchable" class of Hindu that you find such a variety of types. Blind eyes, scars, and the like, resulting from disease and the ravages of extreme fanaticism. Usually the males wear moustaches and beards, matted and unclean.

The Fakir, on the other hand, is a step upward in the caste system.

The old-time Turk wore a fez. The women wore long veils showing the eyes only, the rest of the face and head being completely covered by head-dress and veil. For these characters you have the choice of Olive, Oriental, East Indian, Arab, Hindu, or even yellowish flesh (for old age), for foundation grease paint. All shadows and wrinkles are indicated by means of a warm brown, with bold application. The high-lighting is done in yellow, carefully blended, but for high bridged noses, prominent cheek-bones and chins, the *center* of the highlight is stronger in color, as is the edge of the highlight directly next to the wrinkle or depression shadow. Furrows, crows-feet, age lines, "dissipated" eye effects can be applied if desired. Here is a good chance for effective make-up. The hair should be very dark brown or black. This includes eyebrows and wigs, except for old age types. For scars and facial growths see page 67. The lower castes wear untrimmed beards. Fig. 34a. The higher classes, merchants, shieks, Bedouins, etc. are neat, and trim their beards. Fig. 34a. For the exposed body use liquid foundation to match face make-up foundation.

PIRATES

Figs. 51 & 52

For foundation, use dark sunburn, Spanish, Mexican, dark olive or East Indian. For nose see Figs. 36 & 54b. For eyebrows see Figs. 25c, d. For scars see pages 66 & 67.

Block out teeth, Fig. 56a; use gray liner on chin and jaws to suggest "heavy unshaven" beard. Make lips heavy with maroon liner, turn corners of mouth down. All lining in warm brown, highlights in yellow. Wide latitude is given for the use of red noses and cheeks. The chest may be made up by drawing a design on the chest or arms in blue and red, simulating tattoo. Draw on lightly, dust with powder to set the tattoo.

CONVENTIONAL OLD MAID

Fig. 34c

This type, highly conventionalized, is often used in plays and I think it important enough to give it classification. Comb

EYEBROWS
IN CHARACTER

25 MEPHISTO OR DEVIL

25a SHAGGY EYE BROWS IN WHITE FOR OLD AGE CHARACTERS; IN BLACK FOR ANY SEVERE CHARACTER.

25b CHINESE

25c IGNORANCE, BRUTAL, DEGRADED.

25d BRUTE, IRATE CHARACTER

25e SAD, SAINT, ILLNESS WITH PAIN.

25f IDIOCY, BURLESQUE TRAMP, IMP, ELF.

25g ARCHED, NATURAL, ELONGATED.

✱ DOTTED LINES SHOW ORIGINAL EYE BROW BLOCKED OUT

FIG. 25. *Very important is the treatment of eyebrows.*

FIG. 26. *Elementary application of crepe hair*

Additional details in the application of crepe hair

FIG. 29. MR. WILLARD CARY

In the Author's make-up as Abraham Lincoln.

FIG. 28. MR. WILLARD CARY

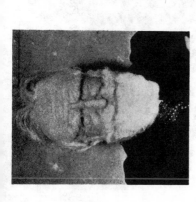

FIG. 27. *A good photo of George Bernard Shaw. But this is not the noted playwright. It is* MR. WILLARD CARY.

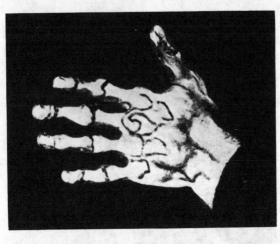

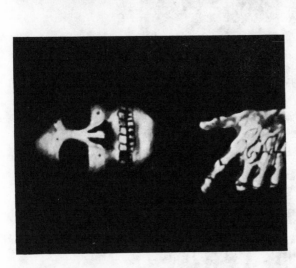

FIG. 30. SKELETON (Death)

The Author's Face made up as a skull. Mustache blocked out. Teeth drawn on upper lip. Besides his own make-up, the Author directed the lighting to achieve this effect.

FIG. 31. SKELETON HAND

Hands often neglected in the art of make-up should receive the same attention as the face.

FIG. 32. MANDARIN

The Author in his own make-up of a Chinese character so often misinterpreted.

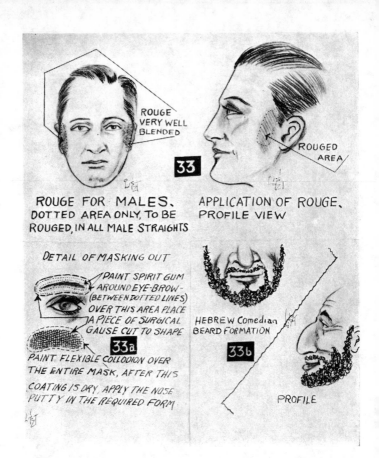

ROUGE VERY WELL BLENDED

33

ROUGE FOR MALES.
DOTTED AREA ONLY, TO BE
ROUGED, IN ALL MALE STRAIGHTS

ROUGED AREA

APPLICATION OF ROUGE.
PROFILE VIEW

DETAIL OF MASKING OUT

PAINT SPIRIT GUM
AROUND EYE-BROW -
(BETWEEN DOTTED LINES)
OVER THIS AREA PLACE
A PIECE OF SURGICAL
GAUSE CUT TO SHAPE

33a

PAINT FLEXIBLE COLLODION OVER
THE ENTIRE MASK, AFTER THIS

COATING IS DRY, APPLY THE NOSE
PUTTY IN THE REQUIRED FORM.

HEBREW Comedian
BEARD FORMATION

33b

PROFILE

FIG. 33. *Rouging of males' cheeks is optional. The older the male (straight) the less the rouge.*

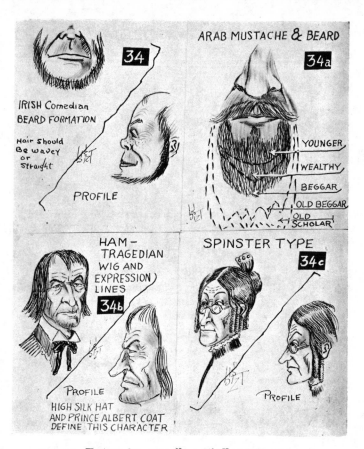

FIG. 34. *Types classed as "caricatures" in make-up*

WRINKLING For OLD AGE.

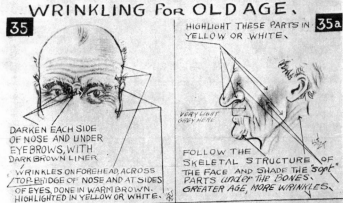

35

35a HIGHLIGHT THESE PARTS IN YELLOW OR WHITE.

VERY LIGHT GREY HERE

DARKEN EACH SIDE OF NOSE AND UNDER EYE BROWS, WITH DARK BROWN LINER

WRINKLES ON FOREHEAD, ACROSS TOP BRIDGE OF NOSE AND AT SIDES OF EYES, DONE IN WARM BROWN. HIGHLIGHTED IN YELLOW OR WHITE.

FOLLOW THE SKELETAL STRUCTURE OF THE FACE AND SHADE THE "soft" PARTS *under the bones*. GREATER AGE, MORE WRINKLES.

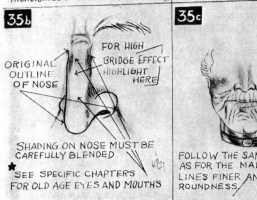

35b

ORIGINAL OUTLINE OF NOSE

FOR HIGH BRIDGE EFFECT HIGHLIGHT HERE

SHADING ON NOSE MUST BE CAREFULLY BLENDED

★ SEE SPECIFIC CHAPTERS FOR OLD AGE EYES AND MOUTHS

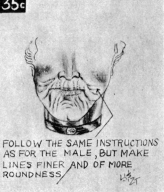

35c

FOLLOW THE SAME INSTRUCTIONS AS FOR THE MALE, BUT MAKE LINES FINER AND OF MORE ROUNDNESS

FIG. 35. *Follow all arrows carefully*

hair, parted in the center, tight down on each side, but let the ears show. Curls may be used in front of ears and on nape of neck. A pug or "bun" should sit on the top of the head at the back. Light pink or yellowish flesh foundation. Highlight the nose all the way to the tip, and shadow each side to make it sharp and long. Thin lips are usual, not brightly rouged. Show the beginning of facial wrinkles about mouth, eyes and on forehead. If the type called for is haughty, make high eyebrows, well curved. If the type is cross and meddlesome, see Fig. 25d. For the pleasant, congenial type, use an old pair of small lens glasses or nose glasses. If the neck is visible show wrinkles and lines at sides, below the jaw lines.

BUTLERS

English type. Sallow foundation, lining in warm brown. Rouge is optional. To define the mouth draw a line on each side of the face from the nostrils down to the mouth. Define the chin by shadowing under the lip horizontally. Crow-foot the eyes and highlight. For side-burns see Fig. 26f. No rouge.

MEXICAN, SPANISH, LATIN-AMERICAN TYPES

Males. Light olive, Gipsy, dark sunburn, sallow or Mulatto foundation. Bear in mind, though this classification appears specific, that there are a number of "mixed blood" types that offer variations from white to brown skin. It is not uncommon to see in one family blondes with freckles, and others who are brown-skinned with negroid features.

Author's note: Don Juan types. Generally "stylish dressers, polite, suave, good dancers and very much the dandy." The locale, the country, the position in life, are all significant and play an important part in make-up.

For the stereotyped Spaniard or Mexican types use the following make-up: olive foundation, no rouge. Lips are made with maroon liner very lightly applied. For side-burns see Figs. 26d, f. For moustache see Fig. 26j-a, & jc.

Females. The Señoras, or married ladies, are generally stout. Women age much quicker in the tropics and young girls of twenty-five often have thin, older hands than we are accustomed to seeing.

The Señoritas, or misses, are gay and stylishly dressed. Latin-American women often make daring and most effective use of cosmetics, and a *white* skin with *red* cheeks and flaming lips is a common sight.

CYRANO DE BERGERAC

Fig. 52e

For a foundation use light sunburn, sparingly applied. The nose *is* the character, without it there is no Cyrano. Nose putty must be used. A sufficient quantity is rolled between the palms so that it is about 3 inches long and 1 inch thick. Start at the top of the bridge of the nose and blend the putty on each side first; then smooth it down until the edges are invisible. Next, with your second finger, rub the putty from the bridge of the nose upward, blending the central part between the eyes until it is invisible. This I call "anchoring the putty." Then work down along the whole section of putty applied, until the required shape and size are secured. When the tip of your own nose is reached carefully work underneath it the extended putty so that no connection can be seen between the putty and the skin at any point. If there is any doubt about the application of the nose putty and the assurance of its being "anchored," apply spirit gum before applying the putty. With the fingers dipped lightly into cold cream, manipulation and shaping will be facilitated. Line and shade in warm brown. A medium, flowing yet rather thin moustache is used. A beard may or may not be used. (Mansfield's photographs show no beard, while Hampden used one.) A shoulder wig is essential.

UNCLE SAM

Use ruddy old age foundation. For nose see Figs. 36 & 54. For eyes see Fig. 42a. For chin see Fig. 26c. Use white crepe hair. Line lightly in maroon and highlight in pale flesh. White-haired wig to the length of the ears should be used. Rouge cheeks slightly. See Fig. 33. Curve the ends of the lips upwards' to give a pleasant smiling expression.

ABRAHAM LINCOLN

Look at the illustration, Fig. 29. Note that I have created a good illusion, because this model did not have the actual facial characteristics of Lincoln. The nose is of putty. The brows are puttied to give them added prominence. Eyebrows were added as explained on previous pages. The mole is added. See page 67. The lines and shadows closely followed photographs of Lincoln. It was necessary to use four different poses in order to get the composite characterization shown. The hair was ironed "wavy" as explained in the chapter on *Crepe Hair* p. 24. In copying noted characters never work from another's paintings. Always use photos, when possible. From these you may make your own drawings in order to clarify the details of the face. Figs. 21, 22, 23 & 24.

GEORGE BERNARD SHAW

See Fig. 27

The same model was used here as for Lincoln, which gives you an idea how facial characters can be "made to order." This model was made up from news photographs. Nose putty was again used. The wig was a "blender" type. The eyebrows, moustache and beard faithfully followed the photographs. Of course, the posture and the Shaw attitude assumed by the model help create the illusion. Every step in this characterization can be easily followed, from the lessons up to this chapter. Light flesh foundation was used. Lining in light brown was carefully done. For modeling the nose a profile as well as a front view photograph was necessary. The nose from the bridge down to the tip was modelled. Be sure of the form, shape and size of the profile. Then came the "front view" of the nose. The nose of any subject must be carefully studied before shaping or applying nose putty.

EDWARD EVERETT HALE

See Fig. 27

Block out eyebrows to follow the natural appearance of the brows and eyes. Use sallow old man foundation grease paint. Add crepe hair eyebrows. Wig as shown is light gray blend wig. Line eyes and forehead carefully and shadow at sides of nose with light brown liner. Care should be given to the hair work here; though the beard is of the grizzly type, the man is neat and clean-looking.

These typical make-ups of living people were given in order that the reader might be "up front" and "see" the procedure of making-up.

CHINESE MANDARIN

Fig. 32

This is a specific type, and should be worked out in detail. The working routine is as follows: Putty nose, Fig. 54a. The real eyebrows of the model are blocked out. Use Chinese foundation grease paint. All lining is light brown, highlighting in yellow. For Chinese eyes see Figs. 42c & 55a. With male characters, do not make the inner and outer lines as definite as for females. Blend and diffuse them. The crepe hair should be ironed and stretched out until it is absolutely straight. Eyebrows are then shingled at a noticeable slant. The two sides of the moustache do not meet in the center of the upper lip. The hair is straight and sparse. The lips should be made in dark maroon, and though full lips are generally required, the upper lip may be blocked out. The chin-whisker should be applied so that it seems to grow out sparingly from the chin. False teeth may also be used. Fig. 32. The hands are likewise made up. For finger nails see page 68. A bald, straight-haired white wig is used. I find that in all Chinese characterizations, by giving the eyes a half-closed appearance, you can usually create the illusion of craftiness, wisdom and slyness.

SKELETON

Fig. 30

There are times when the skeleton role is required. At all events a skeleton make-up may be studied to advantage.

Masks may be used. However, to my mind, the most startling effect is created when the jaws open and the death's-head really is seen, and heard to talk. For this reason I made myself up as Death so that the student, or director, might in a few minutes produce, through the medium of grease paints, a skull that is immediately recognizable and convincing. The procedure is as follows:

1. After the cold cream has been applied, spread white grease paint all over the face, except the eyebrows and eyes and the center of the nose. Smooth over well and evenly.

2. With a black liner blacken the area, including the eyebrows, so that when the eyes are half-closed they will accentuate the natural eye-sockets of the skull. These should be carefully drawn and patted dull with the fingers.

3. With a black eyebrow pencil draw the nasal cavity; you will notice that the septum (cartilage) has been slightly elongated between the two dark areas on the nose. This is done purposely so that the nose will not attract attention and seem tipless.

4. Put the thumbs and second fingers of both hands on both cheeks so that you can feel the last ("Wisdom") teeth in the jaw. But be sure that the lips are well covered with white so that their form cannot be seen.

5. With the mouth closed, draw a line extending on each side over to the last tooth on each side.

6. With a fine-pointed black eyebrow pencil draw the teeth on the upper and lower jaw. (The upper teeth are wider than the lower ones.) It will be found necessary to draw with black

pencil more teeth than actually exist. It is not necessary to duplicate them by actual count.

7. After the teeth are drawn, blacken one or two places on the upper and lower jaws to indicate lost teeth.

8. When this is done "dot in" the sinuses, and with the black eyebrow pencil, draw lightly the areas under the cheek-bones, sides of the nose (back at the bridge) and temples. With the finger blend with gray carefully, to give depth to the areas that need shading.

9. Then draw the lower jaw-bone and fill in the black space below the condyles (temple jaw-bone joints). Highlight in yellow on frontals, front tips and borders of jaw-bones, upper lips and front of chin. Do not powder, but leave the make-up shiny to resemble the glossy surface of bones.

For making up the hands no explanation is needed, as Fig. 31 is clear. Use black liner for the shaping of the fingers and black eyebrow pencil for outlining the carpal bones. Cover the finger nails with grease paint. This is important.

BURLESQUE MAKE-UP

Burlesque characters are used mostly in vaudeville turns, or what is known as burlesque shows, farces and musical comedy. Several of our finest comedians on stage, screen and radio have graduated from burlesque. Don't imagine that burlesque *must* be vulgar; this is not so. Burlesque should be fast, riotous comedy.

TRAMP

Figs. 18 & 19

Tramps may be conveniently divided into the following classes: tramp, hobo, bum. The make-ups are more or less alike, the only difference being that (I quote from Major Bowes' Amateur Hour), "The tramp travels but doesn't work, the hobo travels and works, but the bum does neither." A good tramp foundation may be secured by just applying dark sunburn grease paint and over it thinly applying sallow old man.

This gives a color of out-of-doors, yet with a tint that makes the character individual. A bald wig is used, with little brown or red hair. After applying the grease paint smoothly, block out eyebrows. Putty the nose as in Fig. 54d. Erase both lips with the foundation grease paint color, Fig. 18.

In making a black eye proceed as follows:

1. Apply dark blue liner to top of and below the eye. Blend the blue so that it only covers the half of the eye nearest the nose.

2. From the inner corner of the eye down in a half-circle, following the contour of the lower lid, apply red liner very lightly.

3. Blend the red into the blue so that the red is visible to only a part of the blued area.

4. Below the blue and the red carefully apply green liner, following the same contour.

5. Finally, where the "rings under the eyes" would appear, make a thin line with brown liner. Blend all these carefully so that each color is seen but not separated one from the other. The diffusion of these colors properly done will give a startling and hilarious effect.

On the treatment of crepe hair for this character see Fig. 17c. For eyebrows see Fig. 25f. The unshaven effect of the beard can be produced in the following ways, if desired, instead of using cut-crepe hair. Apply gray liner to the unshaven area. Be sure to cover the area under the jaws and chin, and down the neck to the "Adam's Apple." After the gray is applied squeeze some dark brown grease paint in the palm of the hand and with a small dry sponge stipple the dark brown, very lightly and carefully, over the lightly grayed area. Let the gray peek through. Do not over-do the make-up. Another way to do this, is to stipple carefully with a brown liner stick over the grayed area and carefully diffuse the brown over the gray.

Under this heading comes the old-time conventional "Ham Tragedian." Fig. 34b. He is lean, tall, wide-eyed, dramatic of gesture, with wide sweeping important stride. His right hand is invariably inserted between the top buttons of his Prince Albert.

Use pale flesh or yellowish flesh foundation grease paint. Line the forehead and eyes, and draw deep furrows down center of cheeks and on each side of nose down past the corners of the mouth. Heavy eyebrows and deep-set eyes. The chin is unshaven. The nose is puttied to a long thin droop at the tip. All lining is done in light brown, including wrinkles. Highlighting is done in yellow or white, depending on the lighting of the stage. Fig. 34b. The hands may be made up, big-knuckled and ungainly; the nose reddened if desired. The whole upper lip and chin are grayed for unshaven effect.

BURLESQUE COP

This type may be red-headed, brown-haired, gray or bald. The make-up is as follows: ruddy middle-age foundation grease paint. Putty nose as in Figs. 54b, d. Redden nose and cheeks. For moustache see Figs. 26j–b, j–d.

BURLESQUE HICK OR "HAYSEED SHERIFF"

This conventional character is thin and sharp-featured. For make-up use sallow old man or yellowish flesh foundation grease paint. Line forehead and face as in Figs. 35, a. Chin-whiskers in gray or white, as in Figs. 17d goatee, 26c. Comb out the end so that it will wave with the movement of the chin. Eyebrows are made as in Fig. 42a, but placed higher on the forehead above the natural eyebrows.

JEWISH COMEDIAN

This old-time conventional character can be burlesqued to a fine degree, yet it is often overdone. Use the following make-up: sallow young man or light juvenile foundation grease paint. Line the forehead and eyes as in Fig. 35. Highlight in white. For nose see Figs. 36 & 54. Make the eyebrows heavy. Use crepe hair on the upper lip, coming down thinly at the corners of the mouth, meeting the beard. Use curly crepe hair, closely cropped beard, (see Figs. 33b) brown or black. Use bald wig, brown or black to match beard, or one with a slight forelock. The lower lip should be made to appear heavy; use dark maroon. No rouge necessary. A tooth or two may be blocked out.

IRISH COMEDIAN

Fig. 34

This laugh-provoking character has not been seen much in the last few years, but it is one of the greatest characterizations of the burlesque stage, and I am including it because it should not be permitted to be forgotten. It is, of course, highly conventionalized exaggeration, like the old-time Jewish or so-called "Hebrew" comedian. Use ruddy old-age or healthy middle-age foundation grease paint. Bald blend wig, red hair. Line the forehead slightly. Line the eyes with upward strokes to give the good-natured expression so characteristic of this type. Lining done with warm brown or dark maroon liner. Highlight in white. The nose may be puttied and reddened as in Fig. 54d. Red crepe hair is used, straight type. The hair is applied as shown in Fig. 34. The whole upper lip is blued lightly, the lower lip is made full, and the corners of the lips turned up. Eyebrows may be applied as in Fig. 25f, using red liner. A front tooth may be blocked out, Fig. 56a.

Note: To burlesque any specific character get your role well pictured in your mind's eye. A beard, moustache, eyebrows or sideburns can always be added. Then you may enlarge the nose or mouth. A black eye may be used, or warts, moles and blocked-out teeth. All these are elements of the burlesque make-up and, of course, exaggerated as to facial coloring, or rouging.

THE MINSTREL GROUP. FOR MALES AND FEMALES

First, the minstrel circle and end men. The end men are the featured actors. The circle is the chorus. An effective minstrel group is never made-up entirely in minstrel black. The end men should be made-up in minstrel black, but the circle or chorus should be in minstrel brown. The mouths of the end men may be individualized in the following manner: one mouth may be made-up as in Fig. 41d; another may have the oval mouth turn up at the corners, another turned down, or be made larger, or more oval, etc. Paint the mouth with flesh-color foundation so that the natural lips are not seen. To make a mouth appear larger a black line may be extended from each side of the mouth where the lips separate to the black on the face. A comic effect can be had by making this area white, using white-rimmed glasses in conjunction with the make-up. Eddie Cantor used this make-up with success. Scare wigs are an asset; these are wigs with the top part made loose and a thread attached to it. Upon pulling the thread that hangs down the back (invisible to the audience), the hair is made to appear to stand erect as in fright.

The circle is made up in brown, as already mentioned, and the mouths are made up much the same as with the end men, but not so exaggerated.

EXERCISES

1. Practice puttying the nose so that you can make it in any form. Remember, the nose must have skeletal structure, and the joining areas be invisible when covered with foundation color.

2. Get a blend wig and apply the foundation so that in your mirror you can hardly (or still better, cannot at all) see the joining line.

3. Practice blocking out eyebrows and adding new ones.

4. Practice altering the eyebrows in connection with lining the brow, so that the expression is changed to suit the character.

5. Copy faces of historical and well-known stage characters. This is your greatest chance to bring out the originality and ability that may be in you.

If you should not get the proper effect don't think it can't be done. Follow the instructions given you step by step and you will ultimately improve your technique. However, you must learn the various ways of doing this. It is impossible to follow the later courses in this book without having at your finger-tips the knowledge in the previous chapters and being able to execute the various make-ups. By way of encouragement to those who at first find it difficult to follow instructions, let me say that I am constantly "doing make-up on my own face" and the faces of others, in order to find new effects and easier and quicker methods of achieving the old effects.

Your next step is the Post Graduate Course.

POST GRADUATE COURSE

You should now be pretty familiar with certain fundamental principles of theatrical make-up so that by following the steps outlined in this book you can easily understand the descriptions given in play-texts for almost any role.

On the other hand, if you are required to "create" a character, you should find little difficulty in doing so. I reiterate the absolute necessity of diligent practice.

To my knowledge, this is the only treatise on make-up where exercises are given. At the same time I have used my best efforts to simplify the instructions and the routine so that with average intelligence almost anyone can become proficient in the rudimentary craft, if not the art, of make-up.

MAKE-UP FOR PHOTOGRAPHY

Commercial photographers, and for that matter all of the better studios, use a certain amount of make-up today. There are many reasons for this.

Make-up (non-theatrical) can be used to improve the looks of almost anyone. Facial irregularities can to a certain extent be "made over" and features that are inadequate in relation to the rest of the face can in many cases be made to suggest the natural, oval or regular-featured physiognomy.

Another term for personal photographs in the theatrical world is "stills."

Our first topic here is the ages and types of models. There are men, women, children and infant models. All these come under the heading of "straights." I stress the following important point: colors used in the theater *cannot* be used for black-and-white "stills," for the following reasons:

1. Rouge must be eliminated.

2. The ordinary rouge used on the lips cannot be used.

3. Blue eye-shadow and green eye-shadow cannot be used.

4. Face powders having any pink in them are to be avoided. The reasons are:

1. Red photographs black, therefore red cheeks would register dark hollows on the photograph.

2. Rouged lips, as above explained, would not look natural in the photograph. They would come out black.

3. Blue and green do not photograph with any perceptible degree of color. In fact, blue photographs as almost white, and green photographs a shade slightly darker.

4. Powders with any degree of red (from pink, flesh, and so forth) photograph darker than desired, and the complexion will not look as clear as it should for commercial photographic purposes.

MATERIALS

The following grease paints are used in black-and-white "still" make-up: Chinese, light tan, medium tan, dark tan, yellow, orange, olive and light cream.

FOUNDATION CREAMS

All these just mentioned are for foundations. No rule can be given for the use of any special color, other than that blondes should use the lighter shades, which make the skin more adaptable to the type. Titians, auburn-haired, and red-heads should use medium shades. Brunettes should use darker shades, such as rachelle or light tan, dark cream-color, etc. In harmony with the above-mentioned color combinations care must be taken to notice the color of the eyes of the subject, because there are dark-haired people with light eyes and vice versa. In this case experiments must be done in order to find the suitable foundation color of grease paint that will best bring out the charm and personality of the model-subject. However, it is fairly safe to treat the light-eyed person as a clear-skinned individual and the dark-eyed one as having a darker skin.

After the foundation is applied the eyebrows are lined very delicately. Extreme caution should be used in delineating the eyebrow, with short, fine separate strokes, so that the piercing eye of the camera will not show that the eyebrow has been artificially arched, elongated or reshaped. Any addition to the eyebrow should be carefully diffused with a stump or the little finger.

EYES

The eyes come next. Shaping and modeling of the upper eyelid is most important. If the eyes are sunken and the optical orbit shows a recess or circles under the eyes, a lighter color foundation grease paint should be applied and blended with great care, so that the two colors used may not show any definite line or difference in shade. Figs. 26g, 42d show the area to be shaded. Shadows are made in warm brown, but for darker shading, dark red lip rouge is carefully blended over the brown with the little finger.

Should the eyes be prominent or of the actually protruding type, cover the upper lids with a very light tint of brown liner. The density of color depends upon the shape, size and formation of the orbit surrounding the eye.

Lining the eyelids should not be done for "stills." Mascara in dark brown is my personal choice, because the eyelashes will take on the necessary depth and quality of color, and not appear hard and made-up. Should any lining be done at all, the outer corner of the lower eyelid should be only lightly touched with black eyebrow pencil, and then blended carefully into the skin.

THE NOSE

The nose is a delicate problem. If you want a narrow nose bridge, the procedure is as follows: at the wide part of the nose, on each side, a very light shade of light brown liner is applied to both sides of the nose, but only at the areas to be narrowed. A lighter shade of foundation color is applied on the front of the bridge of the nose, and blended carefully. Should the nose be narrow, and an appearance of widening be wanted, a lighter color foundation is blended on to the sides of the nose, and the degree of highlighting is entirely dependent on the shape, size and length of the nose. If the nose is long and shortening is desired, the tip of the nose should be darkened.

The following section will be divided into three categories, Male, Female and Children.

LIPS

Male. After applying the make-up do not, as a rule, paint the lips at all. However, should some sort of shaping be thought necessary, use medium brown liner. Caution should be used in not defining the cupid's bow on males. This is most important. Lips on men should give the appearance of *not* having been made up at all. See Fig. 6.

Female. The face of the subject should be carefully studied beforehand. If stills are to be made, careful study should be made of the shape of the eyes, nose and jaw, not forgetting the contour of the entire face area. Dark warm brown liner is used for the lips. If these lips are too thick they may be thinned as outlined in Fig. 41b. In fact, lips are shaped and altered as for "stage" make-up; only bear in mind again that red photographs black, so use a warm brown instead of red. Shape the lips so as to give the most expression to the lower face. *Do not* make the lips more prominent than the eyes. The eyes of the subject should attract attention first, then the mouth. If extra shaping is necessary use a stump covered with the color used for the foundation, and reshape the outline of the lower and upper lips carefully. Generous mouths give character. It is better to improve on the curves of the original outline of the lips, giving the subject a proper "picture mouth" suitable for specific still purposes.

Note: A still is not supposed to be the accurate representation of the individual, but a view of a personality, an enhanced physiognomy, improving on nature wherever possible.

Children. Children's mouths should be well defined, but in no way made-up in the sophisticated manner of the adult. Lining is done in a light brown. Never run the liner out to the full extent of the line of the mouth, since this will add an appearance of age and hardness. Blend the lines that form the cupid's bow so that it is almost lost in the upper lip. It should just be noticed, not actually perceived.

POWDERING

Use light cream face powder. In photography the skin must look smooth, so powder evenly and profusely, patting with a delicate steady pat until the whole exposed area, face, neck, etc., is one even color, and velvety-looking to the human eye. Brush off the surplus powder and mascara.

Mascara the eyelids in brown for blondes, red-heads and titians, and black for brunettes.

Touch up any make-up that powdering has dulled, keeping the tone value of each feature the same, equalized in density and proportion.

Note: If the subject has nicely arched eyebrows, or in fact if the eyebrows are of such shape that penciling is unnecessary, the tip of the brush can be used to good advantage in mascaraing the eyebrows.

MINIMIZING WRINKLES AND CROW'S-FEET

Figs. 9 & 10

In non-theatrical making up for the evening, there are times when wrinkles "less seen are best endured." In minimizing wrinkles, apply the foundation color next lighter in shade to the wrinkled area, and work the color into the recesses caused by the wrinkles. This highlights the tiny elongated shadows caused by the wrinkles, making them much less noticeable.

RESHAPING THE NOSE WITH GREASE PAINT ONLY

36

MAKE A HUMPED NOSE BY SHADING IN BROWN HERE, AND BLENDING A HIGHLIGHT IN LIGHTER COLOR FLESH, YELLOW, OR WHITE HERE.

36a

TO WIDEN OR BROADEN A NOSE, HIGHLIGHT IN WHITE OR YELLOW ACROSS HERE

36b

TO MAKE A TURNED-UP OR PUG NOSE, HIGHLIGHT HERE IN YELLOW OR WHITE, BLEND.

MAKE TWO TRIANGULAR SHADOWS AS SHOWN AND BLEND CAREFULLY

36c

TO MAKE A CROOKED NOSE, DARK BROWN SHADOWS, BLENDED LIGHTER

HIGHLIGHT IN YELLOW OR WHITE HERE.

FIG. 36. *Each character has a definitely shaped nose. Don't neglect a good opportunity by forgetting the proper nose.*

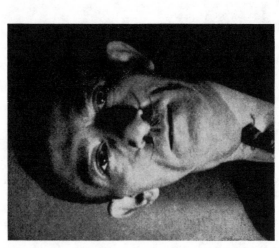

FIG. 37. LIGHTING FROM BELOW   FIG. 38. LIGHTING FROM ONE SIDE

Experimenting with lights is highly recommended

FIG. 39. OBLIQUE LIGHTING

Notice change of expression effected by lighting alone.

FIG. 40. LIGHTING FROM ABOVE

Notice difference in facial structure illusion.

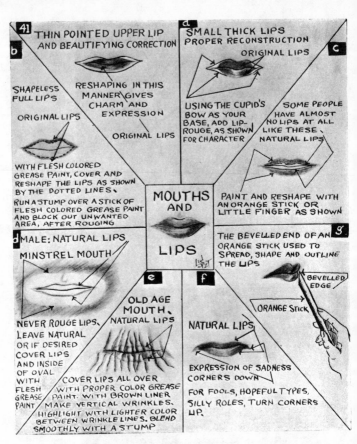

41 THIN POINTED UPPER LIP AND BEAUTIFYING CORRECTION

b

RESHAPING IN THIS MANNER GIVES CHARM AND EXPRESSION

SHAPELESS FULL LIPS

ORIGINAL LIPS

ORIGINAL LIPS

WITH FLESH COLORED GREASE PAINT, COVER AND RESHAPE THE LIPS AS SHOWN BY THE DOTTED LINES.
RUN A STUMP OVER A STICK OF FLESH COLORED GREASE PAINT AND BLOCK OUT UNWANTED AREA, AFTER ROUGING.

d SMALL THICK LIPS PROPER RECONSTRUCTION

ORIGINAL LIPS

c

USING THE CUPID'S BOW AS YOUR BASE, ADD LIP-ROUGE, AS SHOWN FOR CHARACTER

SOME PEOPLE HAVE ALMOST NO LIPS AT ALL LIKE THESE.
NATURAL LIPS

PAINT AND RESHAPE WITH AN ORANGE STICK OR LITTLE FINGER AS SHOWN

MOUTHS AND LIPS

THE BEVELLED END OF AN ORANGE STICK USED TO SPREAD, SHAPE AND OUTLINE THE LIPS

g

BEVELLED EDGE

ORANGE STICK

d MALE: NATURAL LIPS
MINSTREL MOUTH

NEVER ROUGE LIPS. LEAVE NATURAL OR IF DESIRED COVER LIPS AND INSIDE OF OVAL WITH FLESH GREASE PAINT

e

OLD AGE MOUTH.
NATURAL LIPS

COVER LIPS ALL OVER WITH PROPER COLOR GREASE PAINT. WITH BROWN LINER MAKE VERTICAL WRINKLES. HIGHLIGHT WITH LIGHTER COLOR BETWEEN WRINKLE LINES. BLEND SMOOTHLY WITH A STUMP

f

NATURAL LIPS

EXPRESSION OF SADNESS CORNERS DOWN

FOR FOOLS, HOPEFUL TYPES, SILLY ROLES, TURN CORNERS UP.

FIG. 41. *Mouths need much more care than one realizes.
"The mouth is the door of the soul."*

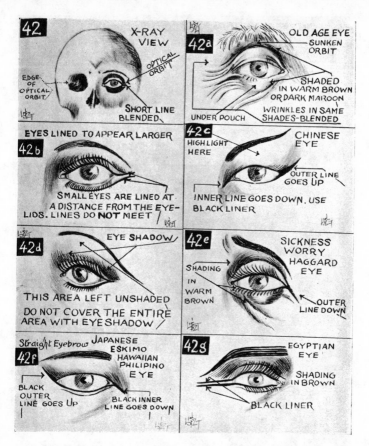

FIG. 42. *Follow the arrows carefully. Shading of the eye is important.*

FIG. 43. SHYLOCK

The Author in his own conception of this famous character in Shakespeare's "Merchant of Venice." Note hand make-up.

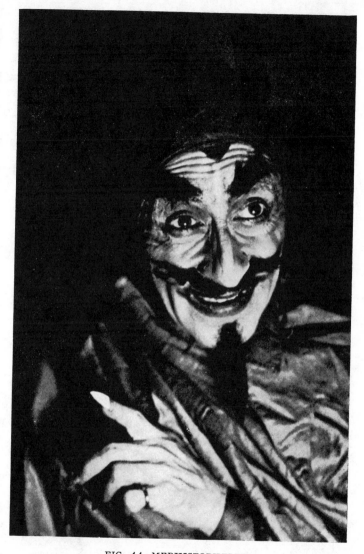

FIG. 44. MEPHISTOPHELES

The Author's example of making putty noses with skeletal (natural bone) formation. Note false finger nails.

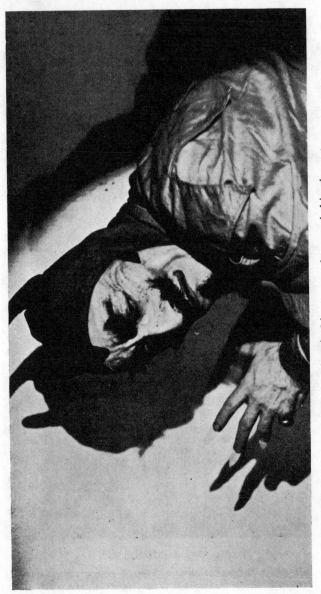

FIG. 45. *The Author in his own make-up of this character.*

This last takes a little practice. It is done this way to produce an effective result without the appearance of make-up. A pleasant surprise is in store for the make-up expert, as well as for the subject, when crow's-feet and wrinkles are eliminated through properly applied make-up.

STAGE MAKE-UP

MAKE-UP CHANGES WITH LIGHTING

There are times when the stage performer has to change in character, or age, right on the stage before the audience, yet continuity in the spoken lines or story itself make it necessary that the performer remain in *full view* at all times. Take for example one scene from *Dr. Jekyll and Mr. Hyde,* as played by my very old friend, that veteran of the legitimate stage, Thomas Shea. He enters, right stage, as Dr. Jekyll and gradually changes to Mr. Hyde, *right before the eyes of the audience.* The bright sunlight gradually changes (and properly timed) finally becomes the well-remembered green light. (Floods.) His hair falls over his eyes, his coat collar is turned up, his hands take on the appearance of taloned claws. How can this effect be accomplished? One good way is as follows: in the straight make-up, juvenile flesh foundation is used. All the character lines and wrinkles in Mr. Hyde are then applied in light orange, unnoticeable in the warm sun-glow floods that suggest daylight. When the lights are gradually changed to green, the hollows, lines, eyebrows, wrinkles, lips, etc., are marked in their change because the light orange is turned to brown by the addition of green light. As brown liner is used for shading and ageing, that same color is produced by the combination of colors made by the orange make-up flooded with the green light.

Should one wish to produce the illusion of changing from straight to minstrel, this is done as follows: the hands and face are made up red, but the red must be of the *same* shade and tone as the *red* gelatine used on the flood lamps. The wide mouth should be made up carefully in a lighter shade red. The *red* gelatine used will make it look as though the performer had been made up straight. Now, change the gelatine slowly to deep blue, and the performer will appear as made up black.

Here are the color principles to be followed in make-up changes by lighting, whereby different effects can be worked to suit the director's wishes.

COLOR TABLE

Yellow and red ....Orange or straw
Orange and blue ....Brown
Red and blue ....Purple or lavender
Yellow and blue ....Green
Green and red ....Brown
Purple and yellow ....Brown

Keep in mind that
    Amber lights absorb browns.
    Red lights absorb reds and pinks.

As above explained, you can now see that make-up foundations corresponding in color with the color of gelatines used, will show straight make-up. Lining must be done in complementary colors such as blues, reds and greens, where amber gelatines are used. By studying the color table you can easily find a complementary color adaptable to the color change required. Eyebrows are always made-up in black, regardless of the color change illusion.

Careful study should be given to colors used in costumes; if decorative or fantastic results are sought, some colors will be lost in the color change.

Finally comes the change from *young* to old, made in full view of the audience. Starting with an orange gelatine, the orange changed for another deep blue gelatine. All make-up is done in yellowish flesh with the lines, wrinkles, hollows and depressions done in orange. The lining may be done in light pale blue if the gelatine to be changed is red. The hands also may be treated the same way. Use two small powder puffs, arranged beforehand, by having them placed in two tins (out of sight on top of a table) containing corn starch. These powder puffs can easily be picked up, unnoticed by the audience, and with gestures (as if brushing back the hair) the powder puffs can be passed over the hair, whitening it, at one time and with one movement, completing the illusion in full view of the audience.

EXERCISES

1. Have photographs taken of your make-up. If you find the results look overdone, you will know that the make-up needs toning down. Your photograph should suggest a living person, not one who has evidently been made up.

2. Get a friend to allow himself to be made up by you, then let her (or him) mix with other people who do not know what you have done. Get their opinions, and profit by them.

3. Get various colors of gelatine (it is not expensive) and practice color combinations. Not only will you enjoy the experiments, but you will find original combinations suitable to your needs.

PROSTHETICS

This section has to do with material additions to the faces and their substitutes for use in make-up. To the student the most commonly known prosthetic is nose putty. Suppose you have no nose putty and you must alter the nose for some special role. Don't worry. You can easily slice off a piece of a stick of grease paint, apply, mould, shape and powder it, and there are you! You have changed the shape of your nose. *But* it must be the same color as the basic color used for the foundation. Mortician's wax, purchased at any funeral home or supply dealer, may be applied the same way as nose putty, moulded and then colored; *but* first apply (and be sure you do) spirit gum to the skin. Cotton batten (surgical cotton) frayed out all around at the edges will serve the same purpose. Place the cotton on the nose and stick it to the skin with flexible collodion, which may be bought at any drug store. Lay the cotton in layers to reach the required height and when the cotton is covered with foundation color, it will never be seen from "out front." The above instruction applies also to chins, cheek and frontal bones.

A good illustration showing the use of nose putty and cotton is my photograph of the Neanderthal Man, Figs. 47 & 48. This make-up took me two and a half hours to remove. The procedure was as follows: first, a proper wig was selected. Then, with sketches, I drew the profiles and front view, masking my eyebrows and moustache as explained. When this masking satisfied me, and stayed "put," with all the natural movements of my brows and eyes there was no reason to fear that the masks would come loose. I then started to build the protruding frontal bones. They had to present the illusion of a low receding forehead. Crepe hair eyebrows were added next, and stuck on with spirit gum. Then I started working on my nose. If you will look at my natural photograph, Frontispiece, you will notice that I have a nose of somewhat generous proportions. With nose putty I built out each side of the bridge so that there was hardly any appreciable difference in depth between the bridge and the sides of it. After satisfying myself with this part of the nose, I started to broaden and widen the nostrils so that I would approximate what scientists believe was the first or beginning of the human nose. (It must not be too monkey-like.) This was accomplished with putty on each side of the tip of the nose, covering the nostrils in width and hiding the natural tip Nature gave me. Next came the cheeks. I first prepared cotton batten as follows: a piece about two inches in diameter was frayed all around at the outer edge; this was stuck on to the cheek-bone with flexible collodion (just as a surgeon does in making a cocoon dressing.) Then, layer upon layer of cotton was carefully stuck in place until I had just the proper area, shape and height needed for this important feature. After the cheeks were completed, I concentrated on the mouth. Nose putty covered the mask over my moustache (and in the case of a smooth-shaven person putty must be used in any case). I built out my upper lip thicker at the base of the tip of the nose in order that the profile should not show the highly developed modern nose, which the prehistoric man of 50,000 B.C. did not possess.

For the upper lip there is very little, if any, of the rouged upper lip known as the "cupid's bow."

Next came the teeth. My own would not do, so I purchased porcelain teeth (of the cheapest grade) at a dental depot, and some red impression wax, the kind used by dentists. The teeth I bought were of the *headless pin* variety. These I arranged on two pieces of adhesive tape, one for the upper and one for the lower set. I then stuck the teeth in place on the *sticky* side of the tape, bending the pins over as they were pierced through, being sure that the lower border, or "biting edges," were free below the lowest edge of the tape. Then each set was covered, front and back, with the wax, which was heated so that it could be formed and properly moulded. These two sets were inserted under my upper and lower lips in front of my own teeth. There was sufficient thickness and curve to these sets so that I could move my mouth (with caution) and at the same time talk with a certain amount of ease and be understood.

The beard came next. Black crepe hair was used and straightened out as explained on pages 24, 25, and applied as explained on pages 24, 25.

Now came the hands. Fig. 48. The fingers were lined for wrinkles and roughness, and the knuckles made to stand out prominently by highlighting them. Instead of applying crepe hair to my forearms and backs of the hands, I pencilled hair lines in the direction of the natural growth of the hair with a black eyebrow pencil, very finely lined.

Here are the make-up properties used:

Foundation grease paint, olive or light tan. Lining and shadowing, warm brown lines. Highlighting before application of hair on brows, frontals, nose and upper lip, with Chinese grease paint, well blended. Lower lip, dark maroon well smoothed down. Tan powder (blending powder) was lightly applied. I carefully brushed off the powder, and the wig was added as a final touch.

Special lighting was used to bring out the effect of the make-up.

UNSHAVEN EFFECTS

If no crepe hair is at hand and a rough stubble of beard is required, you may substitute the black ashes of burnt paper applied over spirit gum—a few cigarettes broken up and the tobacco applied over spirit gum (for sandy-haired, blonde and red-heads) ; pipe tobacco can be used the same way for brunette and chestnut hair. You can also use a burnt cork dabbed on in irregular daubs and lightly smoothed over with the fingers.

If no eyebrow pencil is available, use a burnt match stick.

Instead of rouge you may use red crepe paper moistened, or any cheap red cloth that "runs." You can also use red water-color, but first apply a small amount of moist soap to the skin, let it dry and paint with water-colors. This also applies to any part of the face, eyes, eyebrows, lips, cheeks, etc.

If you have no cold cream and you "must go on" (no matter what happens, in the tradition of the theater, the actor must continue his performance), put on your make-up. It has sufficient "grease" in it so that when you do get time to get cold cream, the make-up will be easily removable, even if you did not first apply it. You can also use any good vegetable shortening instead of cold cream, before or after.

SCARS

Cuts. Red liner, lined on one side with very light flesh. On the other side, lined with dark brown liner.

Burns. Red liner over the required area, highlighted in streaks and smudges with light flesh. Do not powder, leave shiny.

Welts. Lay on strips of nose putty. Cover with a lighter color grease paint.

Old Scars. Cotton batten applied thinly, covered with spirit gum, painted in lighter color foundation cream.

New Gashes. Pull the cheek together to cause a fold, hold together with two thin strips of adhesive tape, top and bottom, laid on across the fold. Dark red liner painted in the crease of the fold. Be sure to cover the adhesive tape with foundation grease paint.

HARELIP

Nose putty applied on the upper lip, blended at the edges all around, but low enough on lip to cover the part of the "red" cupid's bow. With the tip of a stump divide the putty "up and down." Separate the upper lip vertically.

WARTS, MOLES

Nose putty or cotton batten rolled into little balls and stuck on with spirit gum. Crepe hair may be applied on top of moles with spirit gum. Only a few hairs are needed.

BLIND EYE

Use an egg for a model; for a large face use the wider end, for a small face the smaller end. Fray the edges of a piece of cotton batten, lay it over the tip of the egg about a half inch down, cover the cotton entirely with spirit gum, give it two or three coats, letting each coat dry before applying the next. When dry, peel the cotton from the egg. You now have a "shell." With a good-sized pin or wire pierce a hole in the center for the eye to see through (this saves eye strain). Stick in place over the eye, and trim the edges with scissors. Cover the upper and lower thirds of this "eye" with foundation paint, leaving white the middle third, shaped in a horizontal oval. Line the edges with black as if they were lashes, blend with stump. If the junction is visible where the eye is stuck on, nose putty all around and blend carefully to hide these edges.

The above executed and covered entirely with foundation color can be used for an eye tumor.

FANGS OR TEETH

White celluloid, Fig. 32, white cardboard cut irregularly, and spaced and covered with white adhesive tape. These in turn may be covered with transparent adhesive cellophane mending tape.

FINGER NAILS, CLAWS

Fig. 56b

Adhesive tape stuck to the nails, underneath which is stuck pieces of cardboard, making them rigid. Paint flesh color same as foundation grease paint.

Cellophane tape (adhesive on one side) stuck to a piece of pink blotting paper or cardboard, the cellophane left long enough to stick over on to the finger nails. The above are cut to shape as long and pointed as required.

TO WIDEN THE FACE AT THE JOWLS; TO MAKE DOUBLE CHINS

Fig. 55b

Pull pieces of cotton batten, about 2 inches in diameter, and fray all around at the edges. In order to make double chins, start by holding the head way back. For males the face should be clean-shaven and smooth. Begin by laying on one piece of cotton and fastening it with spirit gum. Before it is dry apply the next piece, over-lapping, and extending beyond the first piece. Continue in this way and when the desired area is covered, paint all over with flexible collodion. This will give you a surface to receive the foundation color. Cheeks for the character of Falstaff and such like roles, are made the same way.

FOR MAKING LONG CHINS

Build the chin down and shape the end, as needed, with nose putty. Thus, a Punch and Judy chin, a protruding chin in any form can easily be made. Fig. 50.

BEAUTY SPOTS

The beauty spot was worn by men and women in Colonial days. Today also some European and Oriental women use various shaped (black) beauty spots to bring out the better feature. If the eyes are to be the attraction, the spot is placed on the cheek-bone near the outer corner of the eye. The same rule holds for the mouth. If this feature is the better one, place the beauty spot at a side and below the outer corner of the mouth.

CAULIFLOWER EARS

Nose putty applied to the ear as shown in Fig. 56. This may be stuck behind the ear, colored and blended so as to "double" the ear down upon itself.

TO GIVE THE ILLUSION OF THE LOSS OF ONE ARM

Place the arm diagonally across the front of the body, straight. Lay the hand on the opposite side of the body, just below the hip. With adhesive tape strap the hand to the body, and the effect of the lost arm is perfect, because there is no bulge when the hand and arm are placed in this position properly. Natural body movements are possible.

BEEF-STEAK FACE

Apply nose putty to the lip and continue along the lower edge so that one side of it goes below the lip, i.e. hangs over. Paint with maroon liner, over which blend blue very lightly.

CREPE HAIR—PROFESSIONAL TECHNIQUE

All crepe hair should be treated before applying. The various colors should be washed and ironed so that you have straight, wavy, curly and cut-up crepe hair in every color. Each color should be laid carefully between two thin pieces of cardboard and fastened with paper clips or elastic bands. The hair should be cut into various lengths, from one to five inches. These folders should be filed and kept in labeled order as follows: auburn, black, blonde, brown, light brown, dark brown, chestnut, gray, light gray, dark gray and white.

STRAIGHT, WAVY, CURLED-CUT CREPE HAIR

The tools used for the application of crepe hair are a pair of wide-tipped tweezers, a barber scissors, a wide-toothed comb and an orange stick.

Although there are various mixed colors of crepe hair, at times it is necessary to blend these colors. For instance, at the temple where a wig or the natural hair is gray, and then further down where the beard gradually grows white or darker, as the case may be, blending of the hair becomes necessary.

BEARD TECHNIQUE

Paint the whole area under the chin down to the "Adam's Apple," for full beards, ungainly characters, tramps and patriarchs. Then, with the greatest lengths start at the front under the border of the chin and shingle the hair backward toward the "Adam's Apple," applying shorter lengths gradually. Apply the hair longer than is necessary at first, in order that it may be trimmed to the required length. When the under portion of the chin is finished, start at the front lower border of the chin and shingle carefully up toward the lower lip, as far as necessary, pressing each application down with the orange stick in a horizontal position, carefully rolling it up over the attached ends. Then widen the area along the lower borders of the jaw on each side, until the shape of the beard is as required. The last application of hair should be made with a few hairs at a time so that the top layer may be seen as "single hairs" growing out of the skin.

All the above is done by picking up a few hairs at a time and with the tweezers placing the tips of the hair in their proper place so that it is attached to the skin only where it is supposed to grow. This will permit combing, and result in a beard that can be worn on the street, and practically defy detection. Of course, after the hair is rolled over with the orange stick, and before it is perfectly dry, it should be pressed in place with a soft cloth as in Fig. 26g.

MOUSTACHE TECHNIQUE

With prepared crepe hair about two inches long, start at the outer border of the upper lip, as far as is needed for the character to be portrayed, at the sides of the mouth, and shingle toward the nose (or center of the lip). Remember, lip-hairs grow down. Apply them that way. When pressed into place, dry and comb it in the required direction, trim and fix with the fingers, wax, or adjust in any manner suited to the characterization. Blend the shades that are required to designate the proper age.

SIDE-TAPS, BURNSIDES, ETC. TECHNIQUE

First, close-cropped sideburns or "side-taps." Start at the lower point in front of the ear and work up toward the temple, blending the hair with hair of the wig or natural temple growth. Trim and shape with scissors.

For the thicker, flowing type use fluffy, fuzzy or wavy crepe hair. Start at the lowest point necessary for the type of person who is getting the moustache-attached burnside. Work up toward the temple. As the hair is applied higher on the sides of the face, it is not as long or as wavy (curly) as it is at the jaw or jowls.

BLENDING OF CREPE HAIR

The blending of black and white hairs at times is necessary because of the peculiarity of the wig or color necessary for the age of the person to be portrayed.

First, with the tweezers, apply a few hairs of black or dark brown hair. Over this apply a smaller quantity (fewer hairs) of white or light gray, so that the black hair shows through. Hair is blended in this manner. The colors may be reversed, or any other combination wanted can be worked this way. If care and practice are exercised a *full* beard and moustache of any natural shape can be applied, and the growth will appear absolutely natural.

Be sure to use a good grade of clear, light-colored spirit gum. This substance grows darker with age and exposure to the air. If spirit gum is applied on top of the hair, the result will be a stained and darker border all around the edge of the crepe hair application.

MOVIE MAKE-UP

For the director desiring to make movies of plays, or for technical purposes, the same methods as for stills are used. Ingenuity must be exercised. Lighting is most important in making movie films. For example, notice the two photographs, Figs. 51 & 52. Both have the same make-up. In Fig. 52 you see the scar on the left cheek and below the eye. In Fig. 51 the scar is not visible. This is not the fault of the make-up. The eye of the camera could not register what improper lighting erased. Therefore, in making up for movie films every character must be done carefully and the photographer must place and adjust the lights in such a manner as to get the best possible results. Therefore when making movie shots the studio director sees that there are at least five different cameras grinding at the same time, so that every possible angle is taken simultaneously, and the best photographic result is selected and used in the final film.

MAKE-UP FOR COLOR PHOTOGRAPHS

Most color-films will register colored make-up as applied, but will emphasize the reds and blues.

The safest method is to use make-up as given here in the "Street Make-up" chapter. (Pages 7 to 13.)

Be sure the foundation or powder base is carefully applied. The skin texture must be smooth and uniform in color.

Eye-shadow should be delicate. Blue and green eye-shadows should be applied as a tint, not heavy. Whenever possible (unless there is some special reason to do otherwise) use brown eye-shadow.

Mascara must be used carefully. The eyelashes should not appear hard and stiff.

Lips need special attention, careful delineation; they should be even and symmetrical. Do not hesitate to alter the shape of the lips if need be. Figs. 41, a, b, c. If the lips are moistened and reflect the light, make sure that the photographer does not light the face so that the light reveals the correction. This is a common error many photographers make. (Light hits the lips and the natural upper edge of the lip is revealed. This gives the lip an artificial and made-up look.)

When powdering the face, powder all over, lips and all.

Use the same color, matching it with the powder base or foundation cream. Brush carefully and thoroughly. Good skin-color reproduction can only be obtained by carefully planned application of the colors used.

For Kodachrome, use colors that would be used for evening make-ups.

For other type color films, use slightly stronger colors, warmer, but not over-toned.

Backgrounds. Their color, surface and texture must be considered when making color photographs.

The color of wearing apparel that is close to the face must also be considered. This is most important when considering the flesh color and the placing of rouge.

TELEVISION MAKE-UP

This branch of make-up relates only to "live" talent or what is known as "live video." When telecasting film, the make-up, of course, was taken care of during the production of the film. Television make-up should be more definite and sharper in delineation for good video results. Shadows a bit deeper, highlights a bit brighter.

A modified still make-up is adequate for the general run of Television make-ups.

In the tests, before telecasting, it is best to find out from the camera-man which features are "washed out" or weakened by the lights, and which are not. These features are then taken singly and strengthened, by giving the face depth. This is done by adding shadows in lavender or light brown, and highlights in yellow or white where necessary. This treatment, if executed properly, will take away that flat look so common to most televised faces.

EXERCISES

1. Learn to use cotton batten for the various purposes explained in this section.

2. Block out eyebrows so that they do not show.

3. Apply false eyebrows in various shades and shapes; try to make them look natural.

4. Reshape the nose with putty, seeing that the edges or joining do not show.

5. Make various types of scars. Be sure that they represent the kind of scar you mean them to be. Keep your eyes open

and notice the different skin textures of people in public places.

6. Practice "blind eye" making.

7. Make long natural-looking finger nails.

8. Widen and lengthen the face and practice to get natural skin effects.

9. Practice crepe hair applications and experiment on your friends, seeing if they can notice at a normal distance the fact that the hair is stuck on. If they can, the application is not right.

10. Photograph your make-up. If you look "made-up" your make-up is too heavy, or the wrong colors are used. It is also possible that your lights are not strong enough.

FALSE LASHES

For Stage use, eyes with the aid of false lashes have taken on a dressed up look.

If you find false lashes necessary, they may be bought in most drug stores and over most beauty counters.

The important thing is to apply the lash on the lid at the edge where the natural eyelash grows. That is to say, right under the front rolled edge of the lid and on top of the natural eyelash.

For the most natural look, the false lash should be trimmed, AFTER being applied, so that the outer end of the lash (the end at the outer corner of the eye) is about three eighths of an inch wide, and cut at a slant DOWN to the width of the NATURAL eyelash near the nose. Be sure the false lash is not quite so long (from end to end) as the natural lash at the nose end.

To adhere the lashes, a liquid rubber is used, and this too is available at most drug store or cosmetic counters. It comes in tubes. Apply this adhesive to the "woven edge" of the eyelash with a toothpick.

After the lashes are "set," mascara is employed to mesh both the natural and artificial lashes together. This gives the appearance of thick lush eyelashes, avoiding the artificial made up look.

When removing the false eyelashes, always take hold of the outer tip ends (not the eyelash itself) and pull off toward the nose.

MAKE YOUR OWN

This chapter shows how some of the make-up materials are made. Should the student wish to try them out, he must take care to follow the formulae exactly.

COLD CREAM

Formula A
1 part mineral oil
1 part glycerine
　　　Heat to 150 degrees Fahrenheit
Add while at the above heat and stir till cool.
5 parts water
　　　Heat to 150 degrees Fahrenheit
Add sufficient of any essence (perfume oil) and stir when cool.

COLD CREAM

Formula B

Paraffin	4 dr.
Liquid petrolatum	1½ oz.
Wool fat	1 oz.
Borax	7 gr.
Rose water	1 oz.

Melt the paraffin, add the Liquid petrolatum, then add the other ingredients. Mix.

COLD CREAM

Formula C

Spermaceti	1 lb.
White wax	3 lbs.

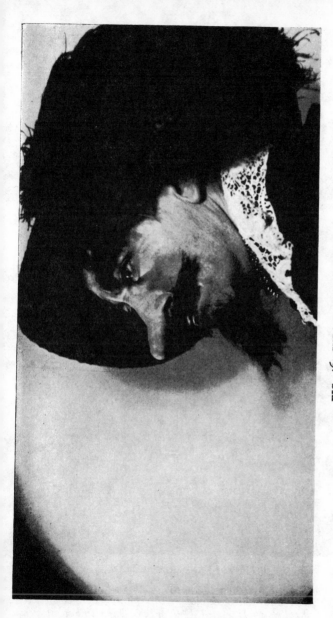

FIG. 46. CYRANO DE BERGERAC

The Author in his own make-up of this famous fictional character.

FIG. 47. NEANDERTHAL MAN

The Author in his own make-up of this character of over 50,000 years ago. The original of this photograph is on permanent display at Harvard University Department of Anthropology and Somatology, in the office of Professor Earnest A. Hooton.

FIG. 48. NEANDERTHAL MAN (*Profile*)

*Here is proof of what can be done by careful study and manip-
ulation of make-up as explained in this book.*

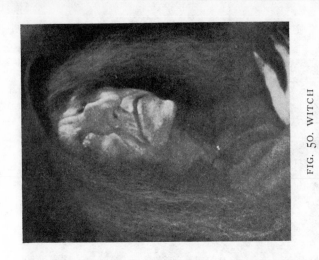

FIG. 50. WITCH

Miss Theresa Robinson made up by the Author.

FIG. 49. MISS THERESA ROBINSON

FIG. 52. PIRATE (*Correct Lighting*)

The Author in his own make-up as a robber on the high seas.

Note: Teeth blocked out—"creped" left eye and cheek, "puttied" nose.

FIG. 51. PIRATE (*Incorrect Lighting*)

Showing "Exposure of make-up."

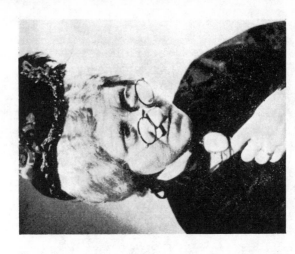

FIG. 52B. *The same Miss in the Author's make-up as an aged lady.*

FIG. 52A. MISS INEZ S. LISZT
Simple straight make-up

FIG. 53. *The Author in his own make-up showing one of many "Trick Effects" the make-up artist must devise for motion pictures*

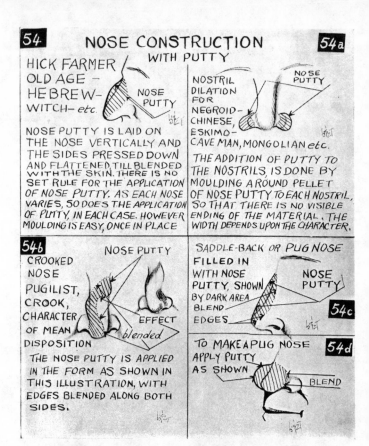

54 NOSE CONSTRUCTION **54a**
WITH PUTTY

HICK FARMER
OLD AGE –
HEBREW –
WITCH – etc.

NOSE PUTTY IS LAID ON
THE NOSE VERTICALLY AND
THE SIDES PRESSED DOWN
AND FLATTENED, TILL BLENDED
WITH THE SKIN. THERE IS NO
SET RULE FOR THE APPLICATION
OF NOSE PUTTY. AS EACH NOSE
VARIES, SO DOES THE APPLICATION
OF PUTTY, IN EACH CASE. HOWEVER
MOULDING IS EASY, ONCE IN PLACE

NOSE PUTTY

NOSTRIL
DILATION
FOR
NEGROID –
CHINESE,
ESKIMO –
CAVE MAN, MONGOLIAN etc.

NOSE PUTTY

THE ADDITION OF PUTTY TO
THE NOSTRILS, IS DONE BY
MOULDING A ROUND PELLET
OF NOSE PUTTY TO EACH NOSTRIL,
SO THAT THERE IS NO VISIBLE
ENDING OF THE MATERIAL. THE
WIDTH DEPENDS UPON THE CHARACTER.

54b
CROOKED
NOSE

PUGILIST,
CROOK,
CHARACTER
OF MEAN
DISPOSITION

NOSE PUTTY

EFFECT
blended

THE NOSE PUTTY IS APPLIED
IN THE FORM AS SHOWN IN
THIS ILLUSTRATION, WITH
EDGES BLENDED ALONG BOTH
SIDES.

SADDLE-BACK OR PUG NOSE
FILLED IN
WITH NOSE
PUTTY, SHOWN
BY DARK AREA
BLEND
EDGES

NOSE
PUTTY

54c

TO MAKE A PUG NOSE **54d**
APPLY PUTTY
AS SHOWN

BLEND

FIG. 54. *A good putty nose is a good sign of make-up knowledge.*

Liquid petrolatum	2 gals.
Borax	4 oz.
Water	1 gal.

Perfume to suit.

Melt Spermaceti and wax. Add the other ingredients. **Mix.**
This formula, of course, can be reduced to lesser quantities in proportion.

ROUGE (Paste)

Zinc oxide	2½ oz.
Bismuth Subnitrate	2½ oz.
Aluminum plumbate	2½ oz.
Eosin	1 dr.
Perfume to suit	2 dr.
Camphor	6 dr.
Oil of peppermint	20 min. (drops)

Dissolve the Eosin in the perfume. Mix the camphor and the peppermint; put together, then add the powders and make into a paste with almond oil.

LIQUID ROUGE [1]

Powdered Carmine	4 parts
Ammonia	4 parts
Rose water	520 parts
Rose essence	15 parts

Keep in a bottle tightly corked. Used with a brush.

DRY ROUGE (Best Neutral Shade)

| Powdered Carmine No. 1 | 1 oz. |
| Powdered Geranium Rouge No. 2 | 3 oz. |

Add a little water to these two, and mix in a mortar to a paste. Let dry in a small tin or mould.

[1] Liquid Rouge is now being offered by some manufacturers as the newest discovery.

SPIRIT GUM

Mastic	1 oz.
Ether	2 oz.
Alcohol	4 oz.

SPIRIT GUM

Mastic	2 gr.
Sandarac	4 gr.
Rosin	12 gr.
Ether	2 gr.
Alcohol	16 gr.

NOSE PUTTY

White wax	8 parts
White rosin	8 parts
Mutton suet	4 parts

Mix together. Color with carmine powder to the proper skin shade.

LIQUID POWDER (Enamel)

| Rose water | 1 pint |
| Oxide of Bismuth | 4 oz. |

Vegetable coloring to suit the shade.
Mix by trituration (grinding or rubbing).

CLOWN WHITE

White meal	2 parts
Almond oil	2 parts
Powdered talc	1 part
Oxide of zinc	½ part

Mix.

ZULU PIERCED NOSE AND SAW EDGED TEETH

55

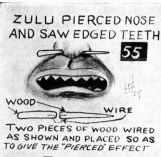

WOOD   WIRE

TWO PIECES OF WOOD WIRED AS SHOWN AND PLACED **SO AS** TO GIVE THE "PIERCED" EFFECT

TEETH

BLACK WAX IS APPLIED TO THIS AREA, TO GIVE THE ABOVE EFFECT

SLANTING EYES MADE WITH ADHESIVE TAPE

55a

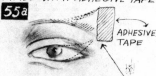

ADHESIVE TAPE

TO SLANT THE EYE FOR CHINESE AND JAPANESE CHARACTERS, APPLY ADHESIVE TAPE AT THE LOWER EDGE FIRST, THEN PULL **UP** AND SMOOTHEN ON THE SKIN. THIS GIVES A NATURAL "ALMOND EYE" TAPE IS GREASE PAINTED ALL OVER

TO WIDEN THE FACE

55b

LAYERS OF ABSORBENT COTTON ARE HELD IN PLACE **WITH FLEXIBLE** COLLODION, UNTIL THE DESIRED SHAPE IS ATTAINED. FLEXIBLE COLLODION IS FINALLY PAINTED ALL OVER THE COTTON, THEN COVERED WITH FOUNDATION COLOR

OTHER MONGOLIAN TYPES

55c

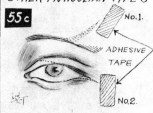

No.1.

ADHESIVE TAPE

No.2.

PULL NO.1 TAPE UPWARDS TO ELEVATE EYEBROW. PULL TAPE NO.2 DOWN, TO GIVE EFFECT OF "MONGOLIAN" LIDS. ADHESIVE TAPES WORK INDIVIDUALLY, AND ARE GREASE PAINTED ALL OVER

FIG. 55. *Note: In the lower part of square No. 55 (teeth) The white section is reversed by the application of black wax.*

Dotted lines show eyebrow and eye lining.

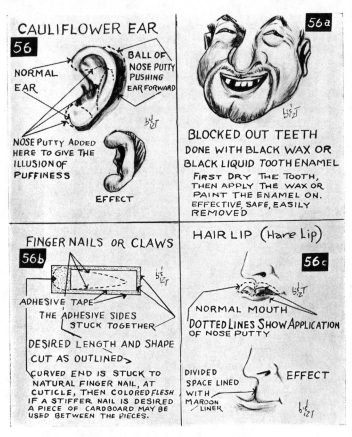

CAULIFLOWER EAR

56

NORMAL EAR

BALL OF NOSE PUTTY PUSHING EAR FORWARD

NOSE PUTTY ADDED HERE TO GIVE THE ILLUSION OF PUFFINESS

EFFECT

56a

BLOCKED OUT TEETH
DONE WITH BLACK WAX OR BLACK LIQUID TOOTH ENAMEL

FIRST DRY THE TOOTH, THEN APPLY THE WAX OR PAINT THE ENAMEL ON. EFFECTIVE, SAFE, EASILY REMOVED

FINGER NAILS OR CLAWS
56b

ADHESIVE TAPE

THE ADHESIVE SIDES STUCK TOGETHER

DESIRED LENGTH AND SHAPE CUT AS OUTLINED

CURVED END IS STUCK TO NATURAL FINGER NAIL, AT CUTICLE, THEN COLORED FLESH IF A STIFFER NAIL IS DESIRED A PIECE OF CARDBOARD MAY BE USED BETWEEN THE PIECES.

HAIR LIP (Hare Lip)
56c

NORMAL MOUTH

DOTTED LINES SHOW APPLICATION OF NOSE PUTTY

DIVIDED SPACE LINED WITH MAROON LINER

EFFECT

FIG. 56. *Prosthetics is an interesting department in the art of make-up. Inventiveness counts.*

MINSTREL BLACK

Beat the lamp black into a stiff paste with glycerine. When using, add a little water, and apply moist. This minstrel black will dry on the face dull and smooth. Removable by washing off with soap and water.

CLEANSING AND ASTRINGENT LOTION

A good astringent, for cleansing the face, and for the application before and after the use of make-up.

One pint of Witch Hazel.

One half teaspoon of Compound Tincture of Benzoine dissolved into one teaspoon of Alcohol.

Add the Benzoine, and one drop of any perfume desired.

Shake well. Apply on a piece of cotton, not with a sponge.

KISS-PROOFING LIPS

1. Apply lip rouge or lipstick and shape the lips.
2. Powder profusely.
3. Brush powder off and moisten lips with tongue.
4. Re-apply lip rouge or lipstick.
5. Powder again and brush off once more.
6. Moisten lips with tongue.
7. Blot with facial tissue by pressing tissue over lips.
   (Do Not Rub)

The above procedure is carried out to permit actual kissing scenes with no "kiss and tell" transfer of lipstick from "she to he."

"AT A GLANCE" MAKE-UP CHART

EXPLANATION OF ABBREVIATIONS IN CHART ON FOLLOWING PAGES

"S" Stands for STRAIGHT
"O.A." Stands for OLD AGE
"Juv." Stands for JUVENILE
"Dk." Stands for DARK
"Fl." Stands for FLESH
"Y.M." Stands for YOUNG MAN
"Lt." Stands for LIGHT
"Reg." Stands for REGULAR
"O.M." Stands for OLD MAN

Character	Foundation	Eyes & Eyebrows	Nose	Lip Rouge	Cheek Rouge	High Lighting	Shadows Lining	Prosthetics
ARAB	Dark Olive Arab Gypsy	See Figs. 13, 25d	See Figs. 36, 54	Dark Crimson	None	Yellow or White	Warm brown or Maroon	Eyebrows Fig. 13, 25d Moustache Fig. 13 Beard Fig. 34a
BLOND (MALE) "S"	Juvenile Flesh	Brown	Reg.	None or Medium	None or Medium	None	None	
BLOND (FEMALE) "S"	Light Flesh	Blue Eye Shadow Brown Liner	Reg.	Light or Medium	No. 18 or Strawberry	None	None	
BIBLICAL (MALE) "S"	Dark Juv. Flesh	Brown Eye Shadow	Reg.	None or Medium	None or Medium	Lt. Flesh or White	Warm brown or Maroon	
BIBLICAL (FEMALE) "S" BRUNETTE	Flesh	Brown or Gray Shadow Black Liner	Reg.	Medium or Dark	Raspberry or Medium	None	None	
BIBLICAL (MALE) "O.A."	Sallow O.M. Yellowish Fl.	See Figs. 35, 25a, 42a	See Figs. 36, 54	See Figs. 35c, 41e	None	White or Yellow	See Fig. 35	Eyebrows Fig. 42a Moustache & Beard

Character	Foundation	Eyes & Eyebrows	Nose	Lip Rouge	Cheek Rouge	High Lighting	Shadows Lining	Prosthetics
BIBLICAL (FEMALE) "O.A."	Sallow Y.M. Yellowish Fl.	White Mascara	See Figs. 36, 54	Fig. 41e None	None	Yellow Fig. 35a	See Fig. 35a	Moles or Warts
BUTLER	Pale Flesh	Brown Eye Shadow	Reg.	Maroon lightly	None	Yellow on cheekbones and chin	Brown Liner Gray Liner on Upper Lip and chin	Side-burns See Fig. 26f
CHILD	Light Flesh	Lt. Blue Eye Shadow Brown Liner	Reg.	Light	No. 18	None	None	
CHINESE	Oriental Chinese Yellow	See Figs. 32, 42c	See Figs. 32, 36a 54a	Maroon	None	See Fig. 32	Medium Brown	Eyes Fig. 55a Nose Fig. 54a Hair Fig. 32
CLERGY-MAN	Pale Flesh	Straight	Reg.	None or Maroon	None or Dark	White as required	Brown as required	Side-Whiskers Side-burns as required

Character	Foundation	Eyes & Eyebrows	Nose	Lip Rouge	Cheek Rouge	High Lighting	Shadows Lining	Prosthetics
CLOWN	Clown White	See Figs. 16, a, b, & c	See Fig. 16	See Fig. 16	See Fig. 16	None	None	Wigs or grotesque Moustaches as required
COSSACK	Sallow Dk. Sunburn	Brown Eye Shadow Black Liner	See Figs. 36, 54	Maroon	None	Lt. Flesh or Yellow	Warm Brown	Moustaches or Beards See Fig. 17d (not parted)
COWBOY	Sunburn	Brown Eye Shadow Black Liner	High bridge	Maroon	Medium or Dark See Fig. 33	Very Lt. Flesh	Maroon or Warm brown	Nose See Fig. 36 Moustache See Figs. j-a, j-b-d
CUBAN (MALE)	Spanish Mexican	Brown Eye Shadow	Reg.	None or Maroon	None	Yellow	Warm brown	Side-burns 26d Moustache See Figs. j-a, j-c
CUBAN (FEMALE)	Gypsy Olive	Green or Brown Eye Shadow Black Liner	Reg.	Medium or Dark	Medium or Strawberry	Yellow	Warm brown	Beauty spots if desired
DANE	Light Flesh	Females, Blue Eye Shadow Males, Brown Eye Shadow Brown Liner	Reg.	Light or Medium	No. 18 or Medium	White on cheekbones	Warm brown if necessary	Moustaches Blond or light brown hair

84

Character	Foundation	Eyes & Eyebrows	Nose	Lip Rouge	Cheek Rouge	High Lighting	Shadows Lining	Prosthetics
DEVIL	Pale Flesh or Red	Black Eyebrows Maroon Shading See Figs. 44, 45	See Figs. 36, 54	Medium	See Fig. 33	Yellow or Lt. Flesh	Maroon	Eyebrows Fig. 25 Nose Figs. 44, 45 Crepe hair, Goatee Fig. 17d
DRUNKARD	Sunburn Dk. Juvenile	Maroon Shadow and Liner	Light rouge	Thick Medium	Medium near nose	Light Flesh	Maroon	Putty nose Black eye if desired
DUTCH (MALE)	Flesh	Brown Eye Shadow Brown Liner	Reg.	None or Maroon	None or Medium	None	None	Blond Walrus Moustache
DUTCH (FEMALE)	Lt. Flesh	Blue Eye Shadow	Reg.	Light or Medium	Light or No. 18			
EAST INDIAN	Dark Olive Moor East Indian	Dk. Brown Eye Shadow Black Liner	See Figs. 36a, 54a	None or Dk. Maroon	None or Dark	Yellow	Dk. Brown or Dk. Maroon	Sparse curly beard or Moustache
EGYPTIAN	Dark Olive Mexican Egyptian	Brown Eye Shadow Black Liner	Reg. Straight	Maroon Dark	Males none Females dark	Lt. Flesh Yellow	Warm Brown	Nose Putty to make bridge of nose straight

Character	Foundation	Eyes & Eyebrows	Nose	Lip Rouge	Cheek Rouge	High Lighting	Shadows Lining	Prosthetics
ELF	Lt. Flesh	Blue Eye Shadow Brown Liner	Reg.	Light	No. 18 or Strawberry	White if required on cheeks	None	Putty Points on Ears if required
ESKIMO	Olive Yellow Chinese	Brown Eye Shadow Black Liner See Fig. 42f	See Figs. 36a, 54a, 54d	Maroon	None	Yellow or White on cheekbones and nose	Brown under eyes and cheekbones	Black, straight, short length hair
ENGLISH-MAN BEEF EATER	Sunburn Ruddy Old Man	Brown Eye Shadow Maroon Eye Shadow Brown Liner	Medium Rouge	Medium or none	Medium near nose	Lt. Flesh or White	None	Mutton-chop Side-burns Fig. 26e
FAIRY	Lt. Flesh	Blue Eye Shadow Brown Liner	Reg.	Light	No. 18 or Medium	None	None	
FARMER	Sunburn Tan	Brown Eye Shadow Maroon Eye Shadow Brown Liner	Reg.	None or Maroon	None or Dark See Fig. 33	Yellow or Light Flesh	Warm Brown or Maroon	Moustache or beard as required
FARMER HICK "O.A."	Pale Flesh Yellowish Flesh	Brown Eye Shadow Brown Liner	See Figs. 36, 54	None See Fig. 41e	None	See Figs. 35, a, b	See Figs. 35, a	Goatee See Fig. 17d

Character	Foundation	Eyes & Eyebrows	Nose	Lip Rouge	Cheek Rouge	High Lighting	Shadows Lining	Prosthetics
FINN	Lt. Flesh	Blue or Brown Eye Shadow Brown Liner	Reg.	Light or Medium	Light or Medium	White	Brown	
FRENCH (MALE) "S"	Flesh or Sallow "Y.M."	Brown Eye Shadow Black Liner	Reg. or Sharp	None or Dark	None or Dark See Fig. 33	White	Brown	Moustache Goatee See Figs. 17d, j-a, j-c
FRENCH (FEMALE) "S"	Flesh Lt. Olive	Brown & Green Eye Shadow	Reg.	Medium	Medium	None	None	Beauty-spots if desired
FRENCH-MAN "O.A"	Sallow "O.M." Lt. Olive	Brown Eye Shadow Black Liner	As desired	None or Dark	None or Dark See Fig. 35a	Yellow or White	Warm Brown	Side-burns beards moustaches
GERMAN (MALE)	Healthy Middle-age Sunburn	Brown Eye Shadow Maroon Liner	See Fig. 36b	Maroon	Maroon	Lt. Flesh	Warm Brown	Lt. Moustache See Fig. j-b
GERMAN (FEMALE)	Flesh	Blue Eye Shadow Brown Liner	Reg.	Medium	Medium	None	None	
GERMAN COMEDIAN	Sunburn	Blue Eye Shadow Maroon Liner	Carmine See Fig. 54d	Medium	Medium	White or light Flesh	Maroon	Blond chin-whisker square & short

87

Character	Foundation	Eyes & Eyebrows	Nose	Lip Rouge	Cheek Rouge	High Lighting	Shadows Lining	Prosthetics
GNOME	Pale Flesh Green	Outline eyes with wide Black Liner	Red Green Yellow	Red Green Yellow	None	White Yellow	Blue	Nose Putty Shape Tip of nose to point
GREEK	Olive Sallow "Y.M."	Brown Eye Shadow Black Liner	Reg.	Dark Maroon	None	Yellow if needed	Warm Brown if needed	Thick black moustache Walrus type See Figs. 26 j-b, d
GYPSY (MALE)	Gypsy Olive	Brown Eye Shadow Black Liner	Reg.	Maroon	None	Yellow	Brown	Wavy Long Moustache
GYPSY (FEMALE)	Olive	Green Eye Shadow Black Liner	Reg.	Dark	Medium	None or Medium	None	
HAG	Yellowish Flesh	Green Eye Shadow Black Liner	Thin, Long Pointed or humped	None See Fig. 50	None	White	Brown	Straggly Wig do not overdo
HAITIAN	Othello	Shaded and Lined with black	See Figs. 36a, 54a	None or Maroon (not Negroid)	None	Chinese	Black or Dk. Brown	Kinky Wig (Natives in the "Bush" are Head Hunters)

Character	Foundation	Eyes & Eyebrows	Nose	Lip Rouge	Cheek Rouge	High Lighting	Shadows Lining	Prosthetics
HAM	See Page 49	See Fig. 34b						
HARLE-QUIN	See Fig. 16c							
HAWAIIAN	Hawaiian Olive Chinese	See Fig. 42f	See Figs. 36a, 54a	Dark Maroon	Dark Carmine	Yellow	Warm Brown	Straight Hair Crop Wigs
HEBREW	See Page 52	See Fig. 33b						
HICK (RUSTIC FARMER)	See Farmer							
HILLBILLY	See Cowboy							
HINDU	See Fig. 13							Leave off beard
HOBO	See Figs. 17c, 18, 19							Use straw hat instead of felt
HUN-GARIAN	Pale Flesh	Deep Set Warm Brown Eye Shadow	Sharp	Maroon	None or Maroon	White Yellow	Warm Brown	

Character	Foundation	Eyes & Eyebrows	Nose	Lip Rouge	Cheek Rouge	High Lighting	Shadows Lining	Prosthetics
HUN	Dark Sunburn	See Figs. 25c, 25d	Broad-Short Wide bridge	Lower Lip Maroon	Medium	Light Flesh	Warm brown or Maroon	Light-brown German Moustache (handle-bar)
ICE AGE	Similar to Neanderthal Man but a few steps advanced in the scale. Nose more developed. Forehead not so sloped. Costume accurately							
IDIOT	Yellowish Flesh	See Fig. 25f	Bridge runs into Forehead	None or orange on lower lip	None	White	Gray	Block out 2 upper Front teeth
INDIAN NORTH AMERICA	Indian	Black Well blended	See Figs. 36, 54	Full lips Maroon	Very Dark	Chinese Olive White Blended	Maroon & Dk. Brown	Proper Wig War Paint
INDIAN SOUTH AMERICA	Mulatto Olive Mexican	Deeply Shaded & lined in Dk. Brown	See Figs. 36b, c 54a, d	Full Not thick Maroon	None	Yellow	Dk. Brown	Slight wave in hair also deep, short curly hair
INDIAN WEST INDIAN	Moor Othello Negro	Shaded in black or Dk. Brown	See Figs. 36c, 54a	Dark Maroon	None	Chinese Yellow	Black or Dk. Brown	Bandana head-dress For Females, Full busted Males, thin black

Character	Foundation	Eyes & Eyebrows	Nose	Lip Rouge	Cheek Rouge	High Lighting	Shadows Lining	Prosthetics
IRISH (MALE)	See Fig. 34							
IRISH (FEMALE)	Lighter Flesh color.							Red wig
ITALIAN (MALE)	Same as for Spanish. (Costumes and dialect define type)							
ITALIAN (FEMALE)	Same directions as for male							
JAPANESE (MALE)	Japanese Chinese	See Figs. 42f, 55a-c	See Figs. 36a, 54a	Dark Maroon	None	White	Brown	See Figs. 55a, 55c
JAPANESE (FEMALE)	Yellowish Flesh	See Figs. 42f, 55a, c	See Fig. 36b	Dark Maroon	None	Yellow		See Figs. 55a, 55c
JAPANESE COOLIE	Same as for Japanese only more severe in shading and highlighting Coolie Costume essential to make-up							
JESTER	See Page 39							
JUDGE AMERICAN	Healthy middle age	Brown Eye Shadow Black Liner	Reg.	None	None	White	Brown	Bald Wig, glasses moustache beard or side-burns
JUDGE EUROPEAN	Pale Flesh	Brown Eye Shadow Black Liner	Reg.	None or Maroon	Medium	Yellow	Warm Brown	Court Wig

Character	Foundation	Eyes & Eyebrows	Nose	Lip Rouge	Cheek Rouge	High Lighting	Shadows Lining	Prosthetics
LAMA PRIEST	This is a Mongolian type, pure and simple. Costume draws fine line of distinction							
LAPLANDER	This is a Mongolian type. More wrinkles and proper costume typifies the character							
LATIN	Latin covers Spanish, Mexican, Portuguese, Italian, as well as Central and South Americans							
LUNATIC	Yellowish Flesh	See Figs. 25c, 25f	Crooked or Straight	Enlarged or twisted	None	White	Green or Brown	Male: Tousled hair teeth missing Female: straggly hair teeth missing
MADNESS	Pale Green Yellow	Maroon Eye Shadow Black Liner See Figs. 25c, d	As desired	None	None	White	Dk. Blue Dk. Green	Tousled hair or wig missing teeth optional
MEPHIS-TOPHELES	See Devil. See Figs. 25, 54. Instead of horns a Red Feather may be worn. See Figs. 44, 45							

92

Character	Foundation	Eyes & Eyebrows	Nose	Lip Rouge	Cheek Rouge	High Lighting	Shadows Lining	Prosthetics
MESSEN-GER BOY	Sunburn	Maroon Eye Shadow Lt. Brown Liner	See Fig. 54d	Reg. or Large Lower Lip	Medium	None	Freckles with Maroon	Block-out teeth Red crop wig
MEXICAN	See Latin. Costumes and Locale differentiate the types.							
MISER	Sallow "O.M." Yellowish Flesh	Dk. Brown Eye Shadow White Eyebrows Figs. 25a, c	Sharp. See Figs. 36, 54	None See Fig. 41e	See Fig. 43	See Fig. 35a	See Fig. 35a	Bald, straight-hair wig Gray beard and mous-tache. Blocked-out teeth optional
MOHAM-MEDAN	See Arab. The style of Costume places the actor in his specific Locale							
MONGO-LIAN	Chinese Yellow	Brown Eye Shadow Black Liner See Figs. 42f, 55c	See Figs. 36a, b 54a, d	Thick Lips Maroon	None	White	Warm Brown	Moustache or beard straight hair, thin growth
MOOR	Moor	See Turk for Make-up Process						Hair is slightly curly, short beard

93

Character	Foundation	Eyes & Eyebrows	Nose	Lip Rouge	Cheek Rouge	High Lighting	Shadows Lining	Prosthetics
NEANDER-THAL MAN	See Figs. 47, 48							
NEGRO (LIGHT)	Lt. Brown	This is a "straight" make-up. See Fig. 20						Cotton may be inserted into nostrils if wide nose is desired
NEGRO (DARK)	Othello Moor	This is a straight make-up			None	Straight		Cotton may be inserted into nostrils if preferred to nose putty
NEGRO MINSTREL	See Fig. 41d							
OCTOROON	Hindu blended with Chinese	Reg. according to age and sex	Reg.	See Fig. 41 Dark	Dark			This is a beautiful Female character. Any artifices are acceptable to enhance it

Character	Foundation	Eyes & Eyebrows	Nose	Lip Rouge	Cheek Rouge	High Lighting	Shadows Lining	Prosthetics
OGRE	Olive Hindu Chinese	See Figs. 25c, d	See Figs. 36, 54	Thick Lips Maroon		Yellow to accentuate cheeks	Warm Brown	Low Brow Black Crop Wig Pointed eye-teeth
ORIENTAL	Chinese, Japanese, Tibetans, and the inhabitants of other Eastern Countries							
PAGE (MALE)	Flesh	Brown Eye Shadow Black Liner	Reg.	Medium	Medium		Warm Brown	Page-boy wig. Some pages of the Kings' courts wear short beards & Moustaches
PAGE (FEMALE)	Light Flesh	All colorings and shadings must be in accordance with color of hair Female pages range from Blond to Brunette						Page-Boy-Bob wig
PEASANTS (GENERAL)	Dk. Sunburn Olive Tan	Brown Eye Shadow Black Liner	According to Nationality	None or Maroon	None	Yellow white to sharpen Features	Warm Brown	Moustache, wig. Missing teeth optional. Show scars if role calls for them

Character	Foundation	Eyes & Eyebrows	Nose	Lip Rouge	Cheek Rouge	High Lighting	Shadows Lining	Prosthetics
PERSIAN	Olive Tan Hindu	Brown Eye Shadow Black Liner	Sharp May be humped	None or Maroon	None	Yellow on Nose, cheek bones	Warm Brown Maroon	Thin, straight beard or moustache Black hair and wig
PIERROT	Clown White See Fig. 16c	Gray or Lavender Shadow	Reg.	Black or Purple	None	None	Gray in Sad type	Black Beauty-Spots Clown wig No hair
PILGRIM (MALE)	Dark Sunburn	Brown Eye Shadow Black Liner	Reg.	Well defined Maroon	Dark or Maroon	Light Flesh	Warm Brown	Gray beard, if Old See Fig. 17 (full) Substitute white hair
PILGRIM (FEMALE)	Flesh	As for blonds or brunettes	As for blonds or brunettes	As for blonds or brunettes	None	None		
PIRATE	Dark Sunburn	Brown or Maroon Eye Shadow Black Liner	See Figs. 36, 52, 54	Dark Maroon	None	Yellow or White	Warm Brown or Maroon	Black Eye-Patch Black Moustache Ear-rings Scars, Blocked-out teeth

Character	Foundation	Eyes & Eyebrows	Nose	Lip Rouge	Cheek Rouge	High Lighting	Shadows Lining	Prosthetics
ROMAN	Dk. Flesh Olive	Brown Eye Shadow Black Liner	Straight	Full with Maroon	None	White or Very light Flesh	Brown	
RUSSIAN	Dk. Sunburn Sallow "O.M." Olive	Brown Eye Shadow Black Liner	Sharp or humped	None or Narrow	None	Yellow on nose and cheekbones	Warm Brown	Straight or Grizzly beard, Dk. Brown or Black
RUSSIAN COSSACK	Olive Hindu Dk. Sunburn	Brown Eye Shadow Black Liner	Sharp, humped or crooked See Figs. 36, 54	Lower Lip Narrow	None	Yellow	Warm Brown or Maroon	Moustaches, Beards, Warts, Blocked-out teeth optional
SANTA CLAUS	Healthy "O.M."	Maroon Eye Shadow White eyebrows	Round and Full	Medium	Medium	Red on tip of nose and on cheeks		White Shoulder-wig. White crepe eyebrows, moustache & beard
SCOTCH COMEDIAN	Sunburn	Maroon Eye Shadow Brown Liner	See Fig. 54d	Medium	Medium	White	Maroon	Blond or Red beard under chin optional

Character	Foundation	Eyes & Eyebrows	Nose	Lip Rouge	Cheek Rouge	High Lighting	Shadows Lining	Prosthetics
SHAKE-SPEAREAN	See Figs. 17d, 35, 43, 55b							
SOUTHERN GENTLE-MAN	Sallow "O.M." Pale Flesh	Brown Eye Shadow Brown Liner	Straight or slightly humped	None or Maroon	None or Medium	Yellow or Lt. Flesh	Maroon	White Part-bald wig. Moustache and beard See Fig. 17d
SPANISH (MALE)	Olive Sallow Flesh	Brown Eye Shadow Black Liner	Reg.	Maroon	None or Medium		Brown or Maroon	Thin moustache, Long Side-taps See Figs. 26d, j, a-c
SPANISH (FEMALE)	Olive	Dk. Green or Brown Eye Shadow Black Liner	Reg.	Medium	Medium			Beauty Spots, Ear-rings, Jewels Spit-curls on Forehead or in front of ears
SPINSTER	Sallow Flesh	Lavender Eye Shadow Brown Liner	See Figs. 34c, 35a	See Fig. 35c	See Fig. 35a	See Figs. 35, 35c	See Figs. 35, 35a	See Fig. 34c

Character	Foundation	Eyes & Eyebrows	Nose	Lip Rouge	Rouge	High Lighting	Shadows Lining	Prosthetics
SKELETON	White or Clown-White	Black	Black	None	None	Yellow on Frontals, Cheek-bones	Sides of nose, under Cheek-bones with Gray	See Fig. 30 Line teeth on with Black
STONE AGE	Prehistoric. See Figs. 47, 48							
TAR (SAILOR) CAPE-COD OR DOWN-EASTER	Dk. Sunburn	Brown Eye Shadow Maroon Liner	Rouge or Freckle as de-sired	Maroon	None or Dark See Fig. 33	Lt. Flesh White	Warm Brown or Maroon	Bald Wig Chin-whiskers All way un-der chin
TEMPT-RESS (VAMP)	Dk. Flesh Sallow Flesh Olive	Deep Green Eye Shadow Black Liner	Reg. to Sharp	Carmine Very Shapely	Medium	Lt. Flesh		White tooth Enamel if necessary
TRAMP	See Figs. 18, 19							
TURK	Lt. Brown Tan Olive Gypsy	Brown Eye Shadow Black Liner	See Figs. 36, 54	None or Maroon	None	Yellow	Warm Brown	Black or Dk. Brown beard & Moustache See Fig. 34a
WEST-ERNER	See Cowboy							

99

Character	Foundation	Eyes & Eyebrows	Nose	Lip Rouge	Cheek Rouge	High Lighting	Shadows Lining	Prosthetics
WITCH	Same make-up as Hag. Costume is specific							Long Gray Hair. Fangs for teeth. Long Fingernails Sharp humped nose See Figs. 50, 56
YANK	Same as Farmer. Sharp Features							
ZULU	Othello Moor	Black	See Figs. 54, 55 Same as Negro	None or Thick Dk. Maroon	None	Chinese	Black	Kinky Wig. Face decorations as for Indian. Large ear-rings, Nose-bones. See Fig. 55

INDEX

ADDENDUM 1949

CAKE MAKE-UP

For Individual Cosmetic Use

There are various makes of Cake Make-Up and all are good. Some are more popular than others due to advertised claims. However, for street wear, the important thing is to match or enhance the skin with the color best suited for cosmetic purposes.

Many skins suffer, however, because of the binding factor used in the manufacture of Cake Make-Up. Lately, some manufacturers have added emollients, such as lanolin, etc., to offset the drying effect the binder causes and to make the skin "feel" less astringent.

I believe most of the so called bad or "bumpy skin" is the result of improper, hasty and faulty cleansing of the face and neck after using cake make-up.

It is a fact that, until Cake Make-Up was created, the actor's skin (I mean the stage actor of the theatre, not the motion picture actor) was smooth, soft and in fine condition regardless of age. But along came the motion picture with its complex and costly production, the speed needed and other elements which go into movie making. Cake Make-Up was produced to give a smooth even skin, when panchromatic film was developed, easily applied, and as easily removed. It was then decided to give the lay-woman the benefit of the "skin of the stars," hence Cake Make-Up.

As this is an important part of the use of Cake Make-Up, I will first suggest the method of removing this cosmetic with the least possible danger of "bumpy skin" results.

Wash the face thoroughly, with a COARSE face cloth. Actually scrub the face with soap and water. If you are one of those people who "never let water touch my face" scrub it well with cold cream and coarse cheese cloth. (Soap and water still is best.)

After the face is as clean as possible, go over the face with a wet but not sopping silk sponge.

Before retiring, apply a thin film of cold cream all over the face and neck and go to sleep.

Upon awakening start all over again as instructed at the beginning of this topic.

FOR THE APPLICATION OF CAKE MAKE-UP

I do not recommend the use of rubber sponges. A good vegetable silk sponge is more easily and thoroughly cleansed, and more sanitary.

Select the proper shade of Cake, and with a thoroughly wet sponge apply the make-up, being sure to cover all exposed areas. Do not apply with short thick daubs. Better use long sweeping strokes.

Have each stroke overlap the previous stroke. Permit to dry. With dry fingers, smooth the skin, and, in this way the cake will blend with the skin, and the dull powder look is avoided. It is important that the skin not be masked with heavy application, and that the neck and jaw line are included to avoid the mask look.

Dry Rouge is applied over the Cake Make-Up. When the desired density is obtained, brush-blend the rouge with a wet silk sponge containing a very little bit of the foundation color thereon.

Add eyebrows, eye shadow, shape the lips, and finally mascara the lashes, in the above order. No powder is necessary.

Some cakes are paste-like in content. These are modern versions of stick grease paint, only softer and much less quantity in compact containers, with the addition of popular scents. .

With this type of Cake Make-Up it is essential that an even application result. To insure a smooth skin and even distribution, moisten the fingers and go over the face before applying rouge. Moist rouge is better than dry rouge for this type of make-up, unless, you wish to use powder, which is applied directly upon the base and dry rouge is then applied, after which the same order of eyebrows, eye shadow, lips and mascara. After which, repowder and blend the rouge only.

LIQUID MAKE-UP

For Individual Cosmetic Use

A good many women like this type make-up. It gives a pleasant-looking result where the pores are not large and the skin coarse in texture.

This class of cosmetic has an oily base such as peanut oil or soya bean, and is applied for best results as follows:

Be sure to shake the bottle very, very well. The powder and liquid must be in dispersion. Place a finger over the mouth of the bottle and invert it. The finger is dabbed across the forehead, and the finger is again covered until the face and neck is covered with some twenty-five dabs.

Wipe the hands dry. With dry fingers and palms blend these dabs together until the area exposed is completely and evenly covered, and be sure the pores peek through.

With a matched powder, or powder one shade lighter, cover the made up area, using a wool powder puff. Brush off the excess powder and with this foundation dry rouge may be used; if moist rouge is used, do so before powdering.

TIP

LEG MAKE-UP

If you like the shade you are using for leg make-up, you can use it for making up the face and neck. However, rub it well after applied as this base is thicker than that ordinarily made for face use. Dry rouge is used with this type of cosmetic.

For removal of LIQUID Make-Up and the LEG Make-Up, if used on the face, Cold Cream will be found most efficient.

CAKE MAKE-UP FOR THE STAGE

As you know by now, there are various makes of Cake Make-Up. It is a convenient medium and if used wisely will be found to be highly efficient for use in the theatre.

It makes no difference what brand is used, as long as the various shades used are of the same brand, because of the affinity of ingredients which is necessary for favorable blending or shading. Manufacturers differ in their formulae and absolutely smooth results are difficult to obtain unless the same brand is used throughout.

Cake Make-Up can be used for shading and highlighting in the following manner:

When the basic skin-tone is applied, and highlighting or the cheekbones, chin or bridge of the nose is desired, fine results may be obtained by using two shades lighter. Wipe the desired area with the thin edge of a moist sponge containing the proper shade. When dry, the outer edges of the highlight is blended with the finger into the basic skin color.

When face-shading is required, let us say, for narrowing jaws, reducing double chins, making hollow cheeks, etc., the same process is used, only for this purpose, darker shades are used, depending on the effect required. Generally, from two to three shades darker are sufficient to sink a cheek or narrow a nose. Of course, shading can be used together with highlighting for stronger effects.

Cake Make-Up has the flexibility of super-imposing, that is the application of one color over the other, as long as the first color applied is dry. Like oils, the colors will not run, but will be independent of one another, and definite shapes and colors can be easily obtained.

It is difficult to mix Cake Make-Up foundation with

grease liners for shading and highlighting. It can be done, and is being done by the author. No explanation will give the reader the "know how." This must come with practice. However, I can tell you that the trick is to blend the grease without touching the cake, thus removing the base that was already applied. A stomp comes in handily for blending purposes instead of the fingers.

For those who perspire more freely, I find that a "cake sandwich" is most beneficial. Apply the cake foundation. Let dry. Apply one or two shades lighter of face powder. Brush off. Again, apply the cake foundation all over the powdered area, thus making a "sandwich."

When applying crepe hair in conjunction with Cake Make-Up, avoid applying the cake where the hair will be used.

For the removal of Cake Make-Up, cold cream is unnecessary. A good soapy lather and water is sufficient.

INDEX ADDENDUM 1949

ADDENDUM 1959

HAIR FOR THEATRE AND TELEVISION

Wigs—Toupees—Falls—Switches—Hair Pieces

1. A WIG is a full cover for the head made to simulate a particular style, or period or both. They are made in all natural hair shades for both male and female.

2. A TOUPEE is a "partial" wig made to cover a receding hair line or the front part of the head together with a bald spot. The wearer has his own hair above the ears and all around the back of the head. These are made for men only. The same style comb is carried out to reproduce the "comb" originally grown by the wearer before he lost his hair.

3. A FALL is a "fringe" of hair from 2 inches to 4 inches in width and long enough to reach from behind each ear. Some are made with a colonial queue and tied with a ribbon. These are wide enough to cover the back of the head leaving the forehead to look natural and the "fall" is always worn in an exact matching shade to the rest of the hair. The hairs are woven on an elastic or very narrow tape and are used to create the hair style of males in the Colonial period.

   Females use Falls to create a page boy or long bob effect when their own hair is too short for the character they are playing.

4. Hair woven together at one end only, leaving the other end free and made of long hair from eight to fifteen inches in length are called SWITCHES. They are worn by females in styles to cover the shoulders, in braids and coils on top

of the head creating coronets, buns and chignons. Switches are also worn to create age and period hair-do's of the 1890 era. When worn long over the shoulders the illusion of youth is effected. Be sure to match the natural color of the hair.

5. Hair Pieces are also known as TRANSFORMATIONS. These are particular pieces of hair woven on lace or silk. made in various shapes peculiar to the exact spot required to be covered. They complete the hair-do blending with the natural head of hair and are undetectable. Although made mostly for street wear, females playing straight roles many times find it necessary to employ the use of Hair Pieces.

NOW FOR THE PROPER METHOD OF APPLICATION IN EACH CASE.

1a. WIGS. The male performer's hair is combed smoothly back, flat as possible. The back part of the wig is held by both hands. The head is bowed and the front of the wig is pulled over the head backward.

b. Females. If the performer has a full growth of long hair, fold and pile the hair flat on top of the head and secure with hairpins. Next, wind around the head three or four times with 2 inch width surgical bandage and fasten in place with hairpins. If the hair is short, use the same method. Be sure that the bandage does not show below the front brow line. Fasten the wig at each temple with hairpins.

c. Blend Wig. This type of wig carries a forehead of silk or cloth and a "bald area" from forehead to way back. The wig must fit tightly across the forehead or the browline will be visible. The best way to hide the blendline is as follows: Foundation or base color is carefully blended horizontally, with the finger, filling the slight shadow caused by the material. With a finely pointed maroon or brown eyebrow pencil draw two or three fine browlines above and below the wig blend. Wrinkling the forehead will show where to place the lines. Powder to soften the effect.

d. Another method is to apply spirit gum to the forehead in a thin line horizontally. Apply wig. Press the browline carefully from the center outward with a damp cloth. To remove, do not pull the wig off. Soak the browline with alcohol or acetone and loosen carefully not to tear the material. Acetone is highly inflammable. Keep away from any flame. Do not smoke while using acetone, and keep away from the eyes. If the wig is loose or a bit too large, make a pleat behind each ear. This will tighten the fit. Always order wigs by hat size.

There are two types of TOUPEES. One with the hair growing UP from the forehead such as crew cut or pompadour. This type has a strip of lace extending about one-half inch across the forehead. This lace, when stuck to the forehead with spirit gum and properly pressed, as explained above, renders a union that is invisible. When a part is necessary "ventilating" is done on a piece of flesh-colored silk that has been sewn in place. "Ventilating" is the process of hooking single hairs onto the lace or through silk in such manner as to give the appearance of hair actually growing from the scalp.

To apply: Place the wig, then with the small brush that comes with the spirit gum bottle, carefully apply spirit gum. Press the lace net (that is below the hairline) carefully (and fairly hard) into the forehead—being very careful not to pleat the lace. Use a damp cloth or a piece of silk to avoid shine or glisten caused by the application of spirit gum.

The other type toupees are those seen on television for the most part. They are slightly curled in the front giving the impression of a pompadour or wavy crew cut. The purpose of this type toupee is to avoid the lace net on the forehead, assuring less detection. They have no lace at all, but are held in place by a special "toupee tape" which is a prepared two sided or double sided adhesive—this holds the toupee to the bald spot. In each case, of course, the toupee must blend into the natural hair by exact color match. Wigs and toupees should be handled with care. When not in use they should be pinned to a head block, having been combed and dressed after each time used. A small amount of brilliantine gives life to the hair and holds the hair in place.

FALLS for males are attached by placing the strip of hair at the desired spot on the lower back of the head. The elastic tape or narrow cloth tape lies on the top rear of the skull. When it is in place comb the hair in front of the tape or elastic forward, and then comb backward over the band, and it will be hidden.

For females, the Fall is made so that each end (right and left) comes up behind the ears. Take a few strands of hair on each side behind the ears and make two small (about two inch) braids. With hairpins pin each end of the Fall securely to each little braid. Comb the natural hair over the Fall to cover the "woven weft" and if the colors match, the detection is most difficult, if not impossible.

SWITCHES are first pinned in place on the crown of the head—more than one hairpin must be used for security measures. Then, braids, curls, chignons, buns high or low on the neck may be fashioned to create the style and character desired. Must be carefully matched with natural hair.

HAIR PIECES: These are pinned in place where necessary. Many times well-known actresses find the need for smooth well-dressed hair on each side of the head in front of the ears. These are ventilated and applied with spirit gum and combed back over the top of the ears, blended into the complete hairdo.

BANGS: These may be straight or curled and are fastened to each side of the temple with hairpins. Be sure in all cases where false hair is used that colors match.

SPECIAL NOTICE

To fit wigs on females: After the wig is applied, and should there be any wisps of hair on the nape of the neck protruding from under the wig, use the tapered end of a rat tail comb to poke the hairs up out of sight under the wig.

EYELASHES: The best eyelashes are made of human hair. They are applied with a liquid latex that is sold in tubes.

There are two types of eyelashes; those woven on strips of hair and separate lashes applied, one at a time. The first (on the strip) are the better and easier to apply.

The latex (rubber) adhesive is a thick white liquid which dries transparent. The tube containing the latex has a very pointed small holed nozzle. Hold the lashes with the strip away from you and carefully squeeze the latex (a very fine ribbon of latex) on the strip, apply on the upper lid directly on top of your lashes. Carefully trim the lashes so that they are longer at the outer ends of each eye and slant out towards your nose to the regular length of your own lashes. Be sure the lashes are applied curled UP. Mascara both lashes—upward—blending natural and artificial lashes together.

How to apply READY MADE HAIR PIECES TO THE FACE:
TYPES: Various sideburns, muttonchops, etc.
            Moustaches
            Chin Pieces
            Beards

There are two types of ready made hair pieces for the face: those ventilated on net and those ventilated on silk. The latter are cheaper, but more easily detected.

To apply sideburns: First paint the area in front of the ears with spirit gum. With a comb push the natural growth upward. Apply the hair piece close to the lower edge of the up-combed hair, then comb the natural hair down to cover the edge.

When applying MOUSTACHES that are ready made, smile a wee bit upon application. They stay on much better this way.

When applying Chin Whiskers or Beards, adhere the front chin part first, then under the chin and lastly, if the beard is full, adhere the ends in front of the ears, pulling upward.

SPECIAL TIPS FOR T.V.

COLOR T.V. calls for a highly different group of colors.

As this field is especially different in color tone from any other type of make-up, anyone appearing before color T.V. cameras are made up by expertly trained Television Make-Up Artists. Therefore, this special category will be left untouched. When color becomes more prevalent, chapters in THE LAST WORD IN MAKE-UP will cover the subject of Color T.V. make-up.

For Black and White T.V.—FEMALE:

Pastel lipstick shades do not have the visual depth of color to give character and delineation to the lips. I suggest the medium or light medium red lipstick. They should not contain any amount of blue. Orange content lipsticks will photograph in color tone almost the same as the pastel shades, PALE lips.

Never line the lower lids or mascara the lower lashes. Doing so will result in "Buttonhole Eyes." The very outer three or four lashes may be darkened with mascara, but none closer to the nose.

MALES: Just a touch of a maroon liner on the lips; then smack the lips so there will be no definite outline to the lips other than is natural with the performer. A definitely outlined pair of lips or dark in color telecasts very effeminate.

OLD AGE MAKE-UP. Male or Female:

Remove any lip make-up. Apply foundation or base covering the lips. With a fine pointed maroon or brown eyebrow pencil draw a few vertical hair-like lines over both lips to simulate age creases on lips and chin.

Remember, never over make-up. Always make-up with the feeling that each line, highlight or shadow could be made a bit stronger.

DR. RUDOLPH G. LISZT,

Local 798, IATSE.

INDEX ADDENDUM 1959

HAIR
FOR THEATRE AND TELEVISION

Wigs—Toupees—Falls—Switches—Hair Pieces

MAKE-UP FOR TV TAPE

ADDENDUM 1964

There are very few television shows today which are televised "LIVE." Television broadcasts either filmed or taped shows.

When one looks at a televised spectacular or feature projected clearer and with better contrasts in black and white, they are taped shows. Up to now Ampex recorders and projectors are used with great success. The camera or recorder is a huge apparatus using a special tape which, like a sound recorder, can be played back immediately, visualized and heard. If for any reason a retake is necessary, the show just taped can be wiped off for re-taping.

To acquaint you a bit with the taping procedure let me explain first about the "camera."

The TV camera is *not* a camera because it contains no film. It truly is a FINDER containing electronic picture tubes called Orthicon tubes.

Video cameras have lenses mounted in a rotating turret which permit LONG SHOTS, MEDIUM SHOTS and CLOSE-UPS.

Long Shots take in the complete stage-playing area, using the 50 mm lens.

Medium Shots using the 90 mm lens encompass the artist or actor from just above the knees up—this lens is more flexible in latitude. Close-ups using the 135 mm lens can be focused on the subject from the waist—the chest —or just the head alone which is termed VCU or very close-up.

119

The picture (visual) is electronically captured on Video Tape either in another part of the theatre building or for remote control, a huge truck or bus equipped with the necessary mechanism is stationed out of sight and sound even as far as a block or two away from the camera area. TV tapes can be edited (cut) with the same facility as sound tapes. Of course, visual and sound must coincide, if not, disaster is the result.

In the control room or truck or bus sits the SWITCHER who with at least three monitors before him, through earphones, gets his rehearsed instructions from the camera director stationed on the floor out of camera range but alert to all the action taking place. The switcher pushes buttons which enable the various cameras (there are generally two or three) to pick up their angle necessary for good showing.

NOW LET US STEP INTO
THE MAKE-UP ROOM

We will just talk about the men for black and white telecasting. A good many stars, announcers, etc. have fairly clear skins or are evenly sun-tanned. They can appear before the camera with one bit of attention. Because, no matter how clean or late he has shaved his dark beard will come through and appear darker. Therefore, his beard area may be powdered and lightly brushed or a very thin light colored PanCake or PanStik may be applied to the upper lip and beard area.

Be sure to blend the outer edges into the normal skin with no line of demarcation.

An important thing to take notice of is, most TV stages still use overhead banks of light. These cause shadows under the brows over each eye, under each eye, and at the "smile line" areas each side of the mouth. These areas are treated with lighter foundation also and blended into the surrounding skin areas. If STAGE lighting is used, make-up as you would for normal transmitting conditions.

Women also will need more careful attention in this method area. Flat moles, large freckles are spotted out separately with a pointed sable brush.

Wrinkles, such as crows feet, can be highlighted as explained in other parts of this book.

For makeup for black and white, makeup as you would for live TV only with more care and refinement.

In production procedures, the main or principal characters are given full attention. Extras are looked over to see that female lips are not too light or too dark. Orange, pastel shades and very dark red lipsticks are taboo.

For TV COLOR—VERY LIGHT foundations should be used and coral colored lipsticks. These colors reproduce (televise) much warmer and natural. When rouging the cheeks, do so very lightly. Use light colored rouge. This color will appear darker also. Other than this, rouging is the same as explained in previous chapters.

Remember, UNDER MAKE-UP, never over make-up.

For GRAYING HAIR, there are silver sprays that work exceedingly convincingly. Apply spray carefully over desired area of hair, then comb carefully.

BLOOD when used for color must be a lighter fuller red. However, for black and white a good blood can be simulated with chocolate syrup.

RUBBER PROSTHETICS are now commonly used to alter the shape of noses, oriental eyelids, jowls, scars, ageing eyebags, completely bald heads and other areas needing contour changes.

Double faced TOUPEE TAPE is used for the fast adhesion of moustaches, goatees, sideburns, and other facial hair additions.

A word of caution in closing.

When preparing to appear on TV, be sure you get the opportunity of make-up rehearsal. Do so before a monitor set so that you get a good look at the characters, the shading, the highlights. This should take place at the same time as full dress rehearsal time is called. Thus, you will be able to correct any make-up deficiency. Most skins need foundation. Do not forget to make-up the neck, the chest, nape of neck and areas behind the ears, ears included, and arms. In other words make-up all exposed areas. Here's wishing you successful taping.

DR. RUDOLPH G. LISZT
Local 798 IATSE 1964

INDEX ADDENDUM 1964

MAKE-UP FOR TELEVISION TAPE

ADDENDUM 1969

MAKE-UP PARTICULARLY FOR THE
BLACK PERFORMER

* * *

This part of The Last Word in Make-Up is just that. It is prepared to keep the amateur and professional performer up to date and fully informed. Herewith is added a comprehensive treatise on make-up for the black artist, male and female, including actors, musicians, singers, comedians and whoever finds it necessary to improve their facial appearance while appearing before the public.

In this addendum the reader will find the names and addresses of make-up manufacturers whose products are most exclusively prepared for theatrical, film and television use. Their colors are dependable, giving the results desired.

Makers of commercial society make-up have colors that may be used for eyeshadow, mascara, eyebrow pencil, and some colors used in their lipsticks may pass. However when it comes to skin color foundations for films and television tried and truly tested colors alone should be used.

I was fortunate, being one make-up artist who made up actresses and models for color fidelity tests both for films and television.

Use make-up cosmetics prepared by those who cater to professionals.

Your appearance result is just as important as your talent.

Sincerely

DR. RUDOLPH G. LISZT
Charter member Local 798
IATSE

ADDENDUM 1969

For the Black Performer

126

In my long experience as make-up artist it was my privilege to make up many black actors and actresses for the stage and motion pictures. Later came the era of television and still photography.

I made up such famed performers as, Stepin Fetchit, Savanah Churchill, Canada Lee, Mantan Moreland, Ham Fat, Peg Leg Bates, Tondalayo, later came Cab Calloway, Hazel Scott, Marian Anderson, Ethel Waters, Lena Horne, and for the last ten years or more many of the familiar faces you see on television.

Originally there were theatres that catered to colored audiences exclusively. Performers worked in those theatres both live and appeared in films shown in the same theatres.

Two of the busiest producers of films catering to this segment of the populace were Mr. E. M. Glucksman of the All American News emanating from Chicago and Mr. Jack Goldberg of New York City.

I was engaged by both of these producers for many years.

The following make-up information is released for the first time with the hope that performers needing my experience will profit by same and learn for themselves proper make-up.

There will be some "DON'TS" that at first will seem odd or in disagreement with past practices.

Try first, making yourself up your own way, then use my method and see the difference as you look into your mirror. Use evenly distributed light on each side of your face and an accessory mirror so that you can see your profile as well as full face.

I have felt for some time the need to add to The Last Word in Make-Up a department catering to black performers.

For live stage appearances the reader can still turn to the "AT A GLANCE" make-up chart situated in the back of the book (pages 82 to 100) and can apply the regular colors indicated matching their own skin tone, using a shade lighter or darker, whichever benefits the facial structure.

In a good many cases the following regular stage grease paint colors may be used: ARAB, DARK OLIVE, GYPSY,

SPANISH, MEXICAN, EGYPTIAN, (light, medium, dark, extra dark) OTHELLO, MOOR, INDIAN, NEGRO (light, medium or dark brown) HINDU, DARK TAN.

All the above colors have been standard grease paint (stick) colors for years. Great advances however have been made in make-up materials and methods of application.

There are now cake make-ups used with a moist natural sea sponge. There are stick forms used with rubber or vinyl plastic sponges. There are compressed powder cakes used dry with a powder puff and there are liquid foundation bases applied with the fingers.

It is for the individual to decide which product is best suited for each skin and which results in the smoothest effect with no "masked" appearance.

The main effect before the audience must result in a clean smooth skin with a pleasing live glisten but NOT SHINING as though coated with enamel.

For the stage, live, use the same methods given throughout "The Last Word in Make-Up," substituting the colors given in "SPECIAL COLOR CONTENTS."

It is most important to realize that when appearing before the film or Motion Picture camera or T.V. Tapes you should insist on an I.A.T.S.E. make-up artist and one should be at your disposal in order to give you the advantage of years of experience all to your benefit.

There are many smaller film producers and many T.V. stations that do not or will not go to the expense of engaging a professional experienced make-up artist. It is for situations such as the foregoing that the following make-up hints are given to help you come through at your visual best until the above condition is remedied.

CAKE make-up is made to use with a damp natural sea sponge. See page 108 CAKE MAKE-UP in ADDENDUM.

STICK make-up should not be applied with the fingers. A much smoother skin is obtained by using a piece of foam rubber sponge cut in the form of a triangle for easy application around the eyes and nose.

Most everything now is done in color. The colors range differently for every type of shooting. Black and white film uses a range best fitted for black and white film alone.

The two frame size films most commonly used are 16mm Commercial Kodachrome and 35mm Eastman color. The latter is the size used mostly for commercials, theatres and professional projection. The screens showing larger projections are only for theatre purposes, but use mostly Eastman film.

The 16mm film is used for some television commercials but in most cases for sales campaigns by large companies as sales instruments for convention use.

The smaller 8mm is sold for home (amateur) projection use.

LIVE TELEVISION, where the performance is taped as it is being telecast needs a special range of colors designed specifically for live telecasts.

Before going into the essentials of make-up for the black performer I wish to lay down a few essential DON'TS. It is important to realize that your image on the screen or T.V. tube leaves an impression on the viewer so why not leave the best you can, one which will be recalled with a warm feeling for you.

FOR THE FEMALE HERE ARE SOME DON'TS

DON'T copy any other performer's make-up. Don't follow the crowd. Be your own individual self. Modern good style is that which makes YOU look best. Analyze yourself before a mirror and be HONEST with yourself.

DON'T use the very light eye shadows.

DON'T line the eyes too heavily.

DON'T over rouge the cheeks.

DON'T use lipsticks that are very light in color. Pearly lipsticks weaken your appearance. Light colored lipsticks may be popular because of the manufacturer's sale scheme. They may appeal to many females but in your case they are detrimental to your general facial make-up. A grotesque appearance is the result.

DON'T use wigs that are uncomplimentary to your head shape in general and your facial structure regardless of late innovations.

DON'T forget to match your face and arms with the same color base.

DON'T neglect to make up your neck and chest as well. Continue beyond your jaw line, as well as the inner shells of your ears.

If your eyebrows are heavy, let them alone.

CONTOUR SHADING

We will begin with the WIDE at the temple face.

Apply foundation that is two shades darker to the cheek bones towards the ears. See Illustration #D1.

If the jaws are heavy and prominent, darken with foundation two shades darker. See illustration #2D.

The face that is full under the jaw and chin line needs foundation use two shades darker. See illustration #3D.

Upper eyelids that are puffy are treated with a darker foundation. See Illustration #D4.

If there is a so called "bag" under each eye, highlight the recess (crease) under the fullness with one shade LIGHTER and apply one shade DARKER over this area. In some cases if necessary the highlighting may be two shades lighter but blended carefully. See Illustration #D7.

When the nostrils are too wide to your liking use foundation three shades darker or black eyeshadow on each nostril. Be sure to pat it smoothly into the skin. Now, apply one shade LIGHTER down along the full length of the bridge of the nose, stopping just before reaching the tip of the nose. See illustration #D5.

The tip of the chin can be highlighted with one shade lighter to narrow the jaw line and point the chin.

In cases where the cheeks are too full and you should wish to decrease this area use three shades darker (very carefully blended) as shown in illustration #D6.

WIGS

Wigs are an important factor. They can add or subtract from your looks. Many performers are using African style wigs which if not too exaggerated enhance a head shape. Others use the slick shiney longer falls or wigs, while others prefer curls. Any one of these styles are acceptable as long as they do not seem too artificial. They must look natural.

Many singers use tinted regular style cuts. I do not like to see these with the darker skins. Better to stay with the chic neat black effects.

It is a good idea to have two or three differently styled wigs yet not too far out in style giving away the fact that they are wigs.

Be smart. Look naturally stylish, not over-made-up or over styled unless it is part of the performance.

MALE DEPARTMENT

In most cases men can get away with very little make-up.

Cake form or the dry compressed foundations are aptly suitable to cover the skin evenly.

The important thing is to cover the shaved area even AFTER shaving because on T.V. especially, the beard comes thru visibly and gives the appearance of needing a shave.

Two shades or in some cases three shades lighter may be applied over the beard area and over the upper lip. Powder lightly and go over the entire face with the foundation selected as proper for your color.

The upper lids may be lined carefully and with a very fine black line. Also the outer third of the lower lid. Use a pointed eyebrow pencil.

Lips may be tinted with a maroon lip stick or liner. "Smooth" the lips so that no definite line is visible.

Should a male performer wear a moustache or beard or sideburns take notice that little bare spaces (sparse) must be filled in with a finely pointed black eyebrow pencil.

Facial contours can be treated by following the same procedure as for females. Blend carefully.

Illustration D8 shows where and how the bearded area should be made lighter in color for cover, as explained above.

MAKE-UP SKIN COLORS in greatest use by black performers.

MAX FACTOR

These colors may be obtained in Pancake and Panstik:

Light Egyptian	Negro #1	For all color skins
Medium Egyptian	Negro #2	Chinese
Dark Egyptian	Eddie Leonard	Hawaiian
Extra Dark Egyptian	Tahitian	Indian

M. STEIN COSMETIC CO.

These colors are made in cake and stick forms.

Othello	Light Egyptian	C-11
Light Creole	Dark Egyptian	C-12
Dark Creole	East Indian	
Hawaiian		

NOTE: The above colors used for black and white may be used for color films and live television color taping.

COLOR INDEX

MAX FACTOR AND CO.
1655 North McCadden Place
HOLLYWOOD, CALIFORNIA 90028

Make-up for black and white panchromatic film

Pancake or Panstik

FEMALE

Very light skin	Fair skin	Medium-Dark
4N or 626B	5N or 626B	6N or 7N or 626C

Translucent powder if using Panstik

EYESHADOW	6 or 22 Pancro
LIPSTICK	Clear Red—Lighter colors are usable

MALE

Light skin	Medium	Dark
7N	8N	9N, 10N, 11N or 665 F

Powder if using Panstik

EYESHADOW	22 Pancro
LIP ROUGE	(Moist) T-3

Foundation Colors for 16mm Kodachrome film

Pancake or Panstik

Female	Male
KF-4	KF-7

133

Foundation Colors for Eastman Color and Ektachrome 35mm film

Female	*Male*
725B 725C 725CN	725E 725F 725G
ROUGE Lt. Technicolor	Dk. Technicolor
LIPS 722 722B	T-3
EYESHADOW 7-34 (grey brown)	Brown

The range of foundation shades for this type film is 725 A, B, C, D, E, F, G, H, which run from very light (A) to dark skin tone (H).

LIPSTICK 7-39 photographs as an entirely natural color.

FOR STILLS, MAGAZINE or Posed Photographs the regular society shades of Pancake or Panstik may be used. However apply one shade darker than that of the natural skin color.

LIPSTICKS with dark reds or those carrying bluish tones are taboo.

MAX FACTOR TELEVISION FOUNDATIONS

Pancake or Panstik

FEMALE

	Fair	*Medium*	*Dark*
CTV	3W	4W	5W
CTV	4W	5W	6W
CTV	5W		

MALE

	Fair	*Medium*	*Dark*
CTV	6W	7W	8W
CTV	7W	8W	9W
CTV			10W

EYESHADOW

CTV Grey	CTV Iridescents
CTV Brown	CTV Brown

LIPSTICK

7-22   7-22B   7-28   T-3 See illustration FIG. 33

CHEEK ROUGE

Light or Flame   Dk. Technicolor See FIG.
CTV   Creme rouge with   33
Panstik only   Dry rouge if desired

NOTE: When using Panstik, pat with powder puff, using
translucent powder, brush off. Pancake does not require powder.

Cake make-up in colors that match those used for the face
are used to cover exposed body areas. After applying, let dry
then rub the make-up into the skin to even the surface such
as chest, back, legs, thighs and arms.

When perspiring, use facial tissue to BLOT. DO NOT
RUB or WIPE as this will cause smears or light spots. Use
a clean tissue each time just before facing the cameras.

In cases of profuse perspiration, a new clean professional
size powder puff may be used and in this case as well, BLOT
do NOT WIPE.

M. STEIN COSMETIC COMPANY
430 Broome Street
New York, N.Y. 10013

M. Stein Cosmetic Company recommends the following
COLOR T.V. FOUNDATIONS.

VELVET STICK SERIES and CAKE SERIES
from C-1 to C-12

FEMALE			MALE		
Light	*Medium*	*Dark*	*Light*	*Medium*	*Dark*
C-3	C-4	C-5	C-6	C-7	C-8

Shading in each series two or three shades darker.

LIPSTICK—*Female.*
Video Pink #1, #2, Video Blush #1, #2, Video Red #3, Lt. Med. DK.

ROUGE—Pink Tone #8 moist, #5, #12 dry.

EYESHADOW—Tan, Purple, Brown, Blue, Green, Violet, Video Grey, Silver Blue.

LIPSTICKS for BLACK and WHITE FILM.

Female	*Male*
Video Light	Video Medium
Video Medium	Video Dark
Video Dark	

Face Powders in all colors for matching, shading and highlighting. A line of make-up for stage and screen performers.

LINING COLORS in stick form, all colors for different needs and effects.

STEIN'S GREASE PAINTS IN TUBES:
Indian Brown, Hindu Brown, Mulatto Brown, Gypsy Olive, Negro Brown, Dark Negro and colors for character types.

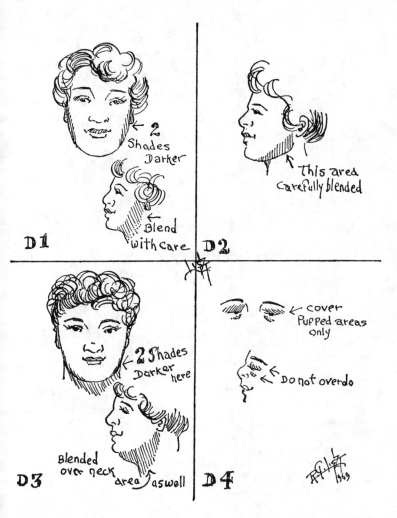

D1

2 Shades Darker

Blend with care

D2

This area Carefully blended

D3

2 Shades Darker here

Blended over neck area aswell

D4

cover Puffed areas only

Do not overdo

A.G. 1969

137

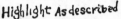
Highlight As described

Dark Shadow on each side of bridge

Side view shading

D5

Apply Darker Shade where lines indicate Shadows and blend out where dots show gradual Fading of Color.
Wear hair Lower behind ears to frame Lower Part of Face.

D6

one Shade darker on puffed area

Two Shades Lighter in the recess UNDER the puffed area. Blend.

D7

Apply two Shades Lighter on shaved areas. cover with regular Foundation Color For males

1968

D8

138

INDEX ADDENDUM 1977
BEARDS, MOUSTACHES, ETC.

ACCESSORIAL MAKE-UP and PROSTHETICS

In the theatre as in other professions progress means change. It also means advancement in techniques. For this reason I feel the following will better the chances of the performer to present a more believable character, and, with less effort.

MODERN CHANGES: The Japanese coolie wears no queue. His hair is shorter, similar to the G.I. haircut. Vietnamese come under this category. Mohammedans may wear moustaches, (Ill.17b) however, beards in this modern era are scarce. Sideburns are being worn. Old men and religious males still stick to the full beard. It may be long crepy or trimmed as in Ill.17d.

Keep in mind the era of the original script and story and do not confuse the modern make-up with the script if the story is set in an era of the past. Be careful. The technique is modern but the characters do not change.

OGRE characters may, at the discretion of the director or performer be scarred, lumpy skinned (page 63) freckled, thick lipped etc.

Since the first issues of The Last Word in Make-Up, theatre lighting has improved, theatres in-the-round are more numerous. When doing Shakespearean characters lighter skin shades may be used with confidence. This means the LOWER numbers and letters in each series of foundations.

Highlighting is obtained by using Factor's "Natural Numbers 1 and 2" (panstik) or Stein's grease stick 1C.

NEW UP-TO-DATE
DO IT YOURSELF INFORMATION

There are many times when the drama student is in need of a beard, moustache or sideburns, therefore he should know how to make one, saving money, time and at the same time enabling him to create a character otherwise impossible.

Here, for the first time in the author's estimation are instructions divulged for the drama student to follow.

Procure a lady's nylon stocking, of the mesh non-run variety. Cut away the complete garter section (top), also the foot part just above the ankle. Cut the stocking open, lengthwise.

Cut a portion crosswise, large enough to reach across the chin area of the face up to and in front of the mid-ear section and under the chin (page 70). With a one inch paint brush that has been well soaped by rubbing the wet brush back and forth over a cake of soap until it is well impregnated with suds, seeing that the brush is kept wet with soap. If allowed to dry, progress will be impeded. Dip the brush into liquid latex and apply over the face where the beard is to be worn. Lay the piece of nylon stocking across this area and press lightly in place with the BACK of a comb, being sure not to pleat or fold the mesh. Any latex adhering to the back of the comb or fingers can be easily rubbed off. Be sure the complete area involved is covered with the stocking and the latex. The laying of hair is next. Wait a few moments for the latex to dry and carefully pull the stocking smoothly from the face and chin. Taking hold of each side at the same time there will be less chance of stretching, and removal from the face and under the chin will complete this part of the operation.

BUT, important is the fact to allow the stocking piece and latex to REMAIN IN PLACE until laying of the hair is to take place to form the beard. The mention above of removal includes the application of the hair on the wet latex. As the hair is being applied the latex might be dry in areas to be covered. Re-wet them with the soaked brush and continue until finished. THEN allow to dry before removing. I repeat the method to be sure the process is well "digested."

After the latex has dried and while the mesh is still in place procure the hair already treated as explained in figures 17 and 17A, 26, A–C and pages 70–71–72. The hair having been straightened or wavy as desired you are now ready to lay it.

1. The hair is applied directly on the nylon on the face as explained above, however, on the upper lips hair in place, apply latex as it is "shingled." See illustration Fig. 17A.

2. As for the chin area. When dry, peel off carefully, being sure to retain the "cupped" shape where it goes under the chin. Powder the complete reverse side with a clean powder brush, keeping the latex from sticking to itself. With a sharp barber shears trim away the curled edges of the mesh not needed. Use care, and if possible cut the edge in waves instead of straight across, as the human eye follows a straight edge more readily than a line which is uneven. Be sure the latex has thoroughly dried before handling or trimming.

Make a slab of plaster of paris by pouring mixed plaster of paris in a cardboard box cover about one inch deep by six or seven inches square, or oblong will do. When the plaster has dried remove the cardboard. Now for an alternate method: Lay the nylon that has been inpregnated with latex on the slab. Shingle the crepe hair in the same manner explained and as each layer is placed as desired, press with the back of a comb, ROLLING the back of the comb UP and AWAY so that you will not pull any hair from the hose that is imbedded with latex.

To make the latex flesh colored, add a drop or two of vegetable coloring (RED) into the liquid latex and stir to evenly distribute the color. The mixture will look lighter to the eye than it will when dry. Again! don't forget to powder the reverse side before starting to apply the hair on the front area.

3. It is better to start with a longer length than needed. This will give you the opportunity of trimming and shaping the beard or moustache into the shape required for the character.

4. When finished, spray both front and back of the hair with a lacquer spray, (colorless). Let dry without disturbing the shape. With careful handling it can be reused. Be sure to remove it carefully holding the outer ends of the mesh ends and not pulling the hair. Start in front of one ear and carefully pull off. Apply rubbing alcohol to the skin as you peel

and this will dissolve the spirit gum as you proceed in the removal. See page 70. If you know how to handle acetone, keeping it away from any heat or flame, cigarette, cigar, or pipe. This will remove the spirit gum more rapidly. Be sure not to inhale while using. Take a deep breath, start removing while exhaling slowly, remove the tissue or cotton with the acetone from the face and repeat the breathing process until the spirit gum is gone. Acetone is highly volatile (flammable) and the bottle must be corked or covered tightly even while using.

For types of beards and moustaches I refer you again to figures 13, 14, 17D, 27, 29, 32, 34, 34A, 43, 44, 47, 48, 52. Other details are given in AT A GLANCE MAKE-UP.

CHARACTER MAKE-UP TIPS
YOU SHOULD KNOW

COWBOY, ROUSTABOUT, the dusty travel-worn character. First, apply the foundation or base. If panstik or grease is used, apply with rubber sponge, if pancake is used, apply with natural sea sponge.

Squint the eyes very tightly, and with a two or three shade darker foundation or brown moist liner sponge (daub) this color OVER the squinted area lightly. Upon opening the eyes a natural dirt-worn face will result. No retouching is necessary.

TO GRAY THE HAIR, there are hair sprays sold in drug stores and beauty product suppliers that come in silver and white. This method gives a more natural appearance and will last longer with no retouching if the hands and combs are kept away. Use the color best suited for the character. Temples may be grayed, front feathered effects can be created. If a character is supposed to grow older during the performance the beard and moustache may be sprayed to show the lapse of years. Care must be taken not to spray the ears or any part of the face or neck. Cover these areas with tissue while graying. The spray washes out readily. Should the spray reach the skin, cover with the foundation in use, but wait a moment or two for the spray to dry. The same spray comes in brown, black, auburn, and blond, saving money and time, should the part call for the color and if the style of hair is the same as being worn, spraying will save the cost of renting a wig, or wigs.

LIMPING, when required may be effected simply by rolling two or three sheets of tissue into a compact ball and wedging it between the fourth and fifth toes of the foot. This will cause discomfort and you will be obliged to limp until removal of the tissue.

SWEAT or perspiration, there is a difference. Sweat is much heavier in appearance. Mineral oil is used to cover the muscular areas, chest and biceps where perspiration and physical dimension is required.

For sweat, prepare a solution of equal parts of glycerine and water in a small plastic bottle with a spray top or any other that will produce a spray easily handled. Spray the forehead, face, neck, etc. This effect is used to help the appearance of toil, fear, exhaustion, etc. Water alone will evaporate quickly but the above will withstand the lights and body heat much longer.

INSTANT BLEEDING. When the script calls for shooting or a stabbing and the subject must show bleeding, there are two methods for producing this effect while facing the audience.

1. For body bleeding, procure a small long shaped toy balloon. Cut the top about two thirds leaving about three inches. Fill this portion with "blood" which is purchased from any of the theatrical make-up suppliers. Wind an elastic loosely around the top of the balloon, yet tight enough to hold yet allowing the blood to squeeze out upon pressure. Pin the balloon under the costume worn in the area to be shot or stabbed. When the action takes place the person shot or stabbed grabs the area (in supposed pain) squeezes the

balloon, or presses the chest with due pressure, causing the blood to escape the balloon and become visible on the costume. If the hand is held in place, pressing, the blood will come through onto the fingers or hand.

2. When a fight is called for and punches are "exchanged" the puncher swings at the victim (your director will give you the action) and blood appears over the lower lip or at the corner of the mouth. This scene is accomplished by holding in the mouth between the lower lip and the cheek a gelatin capsule filled with the "blood." Get the largest size capsule sold in drug stores. Situate it before the action starts, because if held in the mouth for a longer time the gelatin will soften and start to dissolve. The blood does not taste badly and if any is swallowed can cause no ill effects. It will readily wash out of the costume. Max Factor and Steins make and sell blood. There are two shades, one darker than the other. I prefer the darker shade. The brighter shade is made for color films. Both are acceptable, however the choice is yours. The action method is to BITE the capsule at the supposed contact between fist and face and a quick spit out of the corner of the mouth allows for the blood trickle.

Here is an up-dated and modernized "AT A GLANCE MAKE-UP CHART," the colors of which, may be substituted for those in the original printing of The Last Word in Make-Up. Modern lighting, refined and perfected techniques have lessened the variety of colors so that character fidelity is realized and the refinements in film emulsions and T.V. tapes are best accommodated with and by the following.

The original grease paint sticks and tubes have been replaced by materials such as stiks and cakes. They are more easily applied and removed. Faster film and television tapes and improved lighting is the reason.

The chart carries foundation made by Max Factor, but other theatrical manufacturers make shades comparable. I have found that Max Factor's colors are very dependable, constant and reliable.

For the STAGE the "N" series can in most cases be substituted for the "725" series.

The "N" series starts with #1 and goes to #11.

For your guidance here are the equivalents:

725—	A	B	C	D	E	F	G	H			
N	1	2	3	4	5	6	7	8	9	10	11

Numbers 10 and 11 are darker than G and H and are a bit browner because they contain less pink.

SPECIAL NOTICE

Techniques and methods change as improvements take place. Max Factor has discontinued the 725 series in Pancake, but is continuing in Panstik. Therefore for the theatre use the "N" series.

Character	Foundation Stik or Panstik only Color	Pancake Alternate
ARAB male female	Dk. Egyptian Egyptian or Lt. Egyptian	
BLOND male(s) female(s)	725 E-F 725 B-C	N 6-7 N 4-5
BRUNETTE male(s) female(s)	725 F-G 725 C-D	N 7-8 N 4-6
BIBLICAL male(oa) female(oa)	725-C 725-B	N 4 N 3
BUTLER	725-E	N 6
CHILD	725 A-B Natural No. 2	N 2-3
CHINESE	Chinese	Very Lt. Egyptian
CLERGYMAN	725 E-F	N 6-7
CLOWN	Clown	Cake—White stik
COSSACK	725-G	N 8
COWBOY	725 G-H	N 8-9
CUBAN male female	725 G 725 D	N 8 N 5
DANE	725 D-E	N 5-6
DEVIL	725 C	Red Grease Paint-Stik
DON QUIXOTE	725 F See Ill. Nos. 17D 25D 35B 42A	N 7
DRUNKARD (SOT)	725 G	N 8
DUTCH male female	725 E-F 725 B-C	N 6-7 N 3-4
EAST INDIAN	Egyptian-Dk. Egyptian	

Character	Foundation Stik or Panstik only Color	Pancake Alternate
EGYPTIAN	Dr. Egyptian - Very Dark Egyptian - Tahitian	
ELF	725 B-C	N 3-4
ESKIMO	Lt. Egyptian - Chinese	
ENGLISH BEEF EATER	725 G	Lt. Blush Dry Rouge
FAIRY	725 A-B	Natural #2
FARMER	725 G-H	N 8-9
FARMER (Hick, oa)	725 E-F	N 6-7
FINN	Same as Dane	
FRENCH male(s) female(s)	725 F-G 725 B-C-D	N 7-8 N 3-4-5
FRENCHMAN(oa)	725 E-F	N 6-7
GERMAN male female	725 G 725 C	N 8 N 4
GERMAN COMEDIAN	725 G Blush Rouge	N 8
GNOME	725 A, Green Stik-Grease	N 2
GREEK	Very Lt. Egyptian	
GYPSY male female	Egyptian Lt. Egyptian	
HAG	725 B	Natural #2
HATIAN	Tahitian	Very Dr. Egyptian
HAM	725 D See Fig. 34	N 5
HARLEQUIN	See Clown	
HAWAIIAN	Chinese or Lt. Egyptian	
HEBREW	725 F See Fig. 33B	N 7
HICK(RUSTIC)	See Farmer	

Character	Foundation Stik or Panstik only Color	Pancake Alternate
HILL BILLY	See Cowboy	
HOBO	725 G-H	N 8-9
HUNGARIAN	725 F	N 7
HUN	725 G-H	N 8-9
ICE AGE	725 B	Natural #2-N 2
IDIOT	725 D-E	N 5-6
INDIAN (No. AMERICAN)	Indian	
INDIAN (WEST INDIAN)	Eddie Leonard - Negro - very Dk. Egyptian	
IRISH male female	725 G 725 B-C	N 8 N 3-4
ISRAELIAN	725 F-G	N 7-8
ITALIAN male female	F-G 725 B-C	N 7-8 N 3-4
JAPANESE male female	Chinese Chinese	
JAPANESE (GEISHA)	Natural #1	
JAPANESE COOLIE	Chinese	
JESTER	725 C	N 4
JUDGE (AMERICAN)	725 F	N 7
JUDGE (EUROPEAN)	725 F	N 7
LAMA PRIEST	Chinese	Very Lt. Egyptian
LAPLANDER	Chinese	Lt. Egyptian
LATIN	Lt. Egyptian	
LUNATIC	725 A-B Natural #2	N 3

Character	Foundation Stik or Panstik only Color	Pancake Alternate
MEPHISTOPHELES	See Devil	
MESSINGER BOY	725 F	N 7
MEXICAN	See Latin	
MISER	725 B Natural #2	N 3
MOHAMMEDAN	See Arab	
MONGOLIAN	See Chinese	
MOOR	Tahitian	N 10-11
NEANDERTHAL MAN	725 H	N 10
NEGRO (Light)	Negro #1	Very Dk. Egyptian
NEGRO (Dark)	Negro #2	Eddie Leonard
MINSTREL NEGRO	Black	
OCTOROON	EGYPTIAN (over) Chinese	
OGRE	725 H	N 10
ORIENTAL	CHINESE OR EGYPTIAN	N 9
PAGE (male)	725 F	N 7
PAGE (female or) AIRLINE HOSTESS	725 B-C	N 3-4
PEASANTS (general)	725 G-H	N 8-9
PERSIAN	See Oriental	
PIERROT	See Clown	
PILGRAM male female	725 F 725 C	N 7 N 4
PIRATE	725 H	N 9
ROMAN	Egyptian or Latin	

Character	Foundation Stik or Panstik only Color	Pancake Alternate
RUSSIAN	725 F-G	N 7-8
RUSSIAN COSSACK	725 H	N 8
SANTA CLAUS	725 F	N 7
SCOTCH COMEDIAN	725 G	N 8
SHAKESPEAREAN male female	725 C to F 725 B to D	N 4 to 7 N 3 to 5
SOUTHERN GENTLEMAN	725 F	N 7
SPANISH male female	See Latin 725 8-9 See Latin	
SPINSTER	725 B	N 3-4
SKELETON	Clown white with black for recesses	
STONE AGE	725 H	N 10
TAR (sailor) Cape Cod or Down Easter	725 G	N 8
TEMPTRESS (Vamp)	725 C-D	N 4-5
TURK	See Arab	
WESTERN TYPES	See Cowboy	
WITCH	725-B Natural #2	N 2-3
ZULU (African)	Tahitian or Eddie Leonard	N-11

SPECIAL NOTICE:
When making up for character be sure the backs of the hands and other exposed areas are covered with the same color used on the face.

151